TYRANNY OF THE NORMAL

Tyranny
of the
Normal

ESSAYS ON BIOETHICS,

THEOLOGY & MYTH

Leslie Fiedler

DAVID R. GODINE, PUBLISHER

Boston

First published in 1996 by
David R. Godine, Publisher, Inc.
Box 9103
Lincoln, Massachusetts 01773

Library of Congress Cataloging in Publication Data
Fiedler, Leslie A.
Tyranny of the normal: essays on bioethics, theology &
myth / Leslie Fiedler.
p.   cm.
ISBN 1-56792-003-9
I. Title.
PS3556.I34T97   1996
814'.54—dc20
95-34579
CIP

First printing, 1996

This book was printed on acid-free paper

Printed in the United States of America

Contents

In Memory of Irving Sanes

The Atoms of Democritus
And Newton's Particles of light
Are sands upon the Red sea shore,
Where Israel's tents do shine so bright.
WILLIAM BLAKE

Introduction: To You, Whoever You Are

⇒✦✦

INTERLOPER, KIBITZER, DOUBLE AGENT, mole, wolf in sheep's clothing, lion in the Daniel's den: these are the metaphors that occur to me to describe the self who speaks in these essays, which I originally delivered as a generalist addressing specialists. Such ventures have taken me far from the classroom in English Literature, which for over half a century now has been my home ground.

The first of them, indeed, began—improbably enough—as the keynote speech at a World Conference of Theologians, not a few of whom seemed as suspicious of my credentials when I finished as when I was introduced. Another, even more improbably, I delivered at the inaugural ceremonies for the Year of the Handicapped, held at the New York headquarters of the United Nations, where, among bureaucrats with ambassadorial rank, I felt myself not just a hopeless amateur but the ultimate stranger in a strange land.

It was not the *chutzpah* endemic in the young that prompted such forays out of my own territory. Nor was it the desire, common in the old, to find new life in a new subject. Rather it was an unwillingness to preach to the converted that has persisted from youth to age: a yearning to open up communication instead with those outside my own small compartment in the Ivory Tower—to talk to *everyone*. After all, even before I became (more or less by accident) a critic-pedagogue, I was already (by free choice) a poet and writer of short stories. Indeed, though I am now known chiefly for my critical essays, I continue to produce poetry and fiction: works, that is to say, intended not for fellow teachers and students, but, in the felicitous phrase of Walt Whitman, for "you, whoever you are..."

Moreover, before I had learned how to talk to a captive audience from the professor's side of the desk, I had learned, as a political activist, to talk from a street-corner soapbox to any and all passersby. Nothing has ever given me a greater thrill than the immediate responses of such random audiences, whether positive or negative: catcalls and yells of "Who's paying you for those remarks, buddy? Moscow gold?"; or sighs of assent and cries of "Now you're preachin', brother. Go right on preachin'!" For that reason, perhaps, even after I had become an Instructor in English at the University of Montana, I chose to lecture not to small seminars of upperclass majors but to large groups of freshmen and sophomores, most of whom would not make it to any degree. So, too, I headed out in quest of even less elite auditors to whatever little town on the western slope of the Rockies whose book club could be persuaded to listen to me.

Once there, to be sure, I would insist on speaking (over the clicking of knitting needles and the snores of those who fell asleep before I was through) about such books as *Finnegans Wake*, which I was convinced they would never read. In retrospect, those efforts to bring, however vicariously, metropolitan high culture to low-brow provincials strike me as having been rather condescending. But at least in my misguided zeal, I learned how to discuss works prized by the minority in the common tongue I shared with the majority, who find the hermetic jargon of most literary discourse quite incomprehensible.

It took me longer to learn to write in that language, or even to realize that I yearned to do so. Indeed, I was forty years old before I tried to publish any critical essays. When I did so, moreover, I did not submit them to the thick, unreadable scholarly journals in which my junior colleagues aspired to appear. Instead, I sent my earliest efforts off—hopefully and eventually successfully—to periodicals like the *Partisan Review*, the *Kenyon Review*, the *New*

Introduction

Republic, the *Nation*, the *New Leader*, and *Encounter*. At that point, however, my senior colleagues did not consider publication in such extra-academic quarterlies and weeklies grounds for promotion and tenure. Not only did they consider their style too *leserfreundlich*, more like journalism than rigorous scholarship; they also found their Modernist esthetics and their anti-Stalinist politics reprehensible.

But what irked my elders pleased me, since on the one hand I wanted to be read rather than studied or deciphered, and on the other I dreamed of opening the canon to experimental, avant-garde writing in a socialist society. It should not have surprised me then that my first book (a collection of essays I called *An End to Innocence*) was excoriated by proper academics for its critical heresies and by conventional liberals for its political unorthodoxy. I had, after all, not only insisted that at the erotic heart of our greatest literature was a myth of interethnic male-bonding but I had argued that Alger Hiss and the Rosenbergs were guilty as charged.

I must admit, however, that though I was a little dismayed, I consoled myself with the thought that at least my slim volume—in which I had inadvertently invented "Cultural Studies" before it had a name—was read and responded to by some readers ordinarily indifferent to literary criticism. These included a future President of the United States, who disconcertingly wrote one of the few approving letters I received: applauding my piece on Hiss, despite the fact that in the sole reference to him, thanks to a typo, he was called "Dixon."

It was the political dimension of my essays that chiefly attracted such readers; and how could it not at a moment when the troubled outside world it had so long ignored was beginning to invade the campus—in the form not just of demonstrations and teach-ins, but poetry readings by the self-styled "beats." Yet, ironically enough, even as this invasion reached its climax, I myself was losing faith in all politics, which had come to seem to me the new "opium of the people."

Nonetheless, throughout the sixties, I did keep writing about the Cultural Revolution of the young, since despite its political sloganeering it seemed to me essentially as metapolitical as I had become. In my quest for a new audience on both sides of the infamous "Generation Gap," I abandoned the journals dominated by the "New York Intellectuals" with whom I had been originally identified but who, as their dissent hardened into orthodoxy, grew ever more unsympathetic to any attempt at coming to terms with the "New Left." I was pleased, therefore, to discover that a new forum was being offered me (for reasons I never quite understood) by mass circulation magazines like *Esquire* and even *Playboy*, the latter of which I had never read before appearing in its glossy pages.

But of course (as I had all along foreseen, though with a speed I had not anticipated), like all revolutions, that of the disaffected young failed even as it succeeded, failed precisely because of its success. That is to say, it brought about changes its proponents had from the first advocated but which they found disconcerting when they actually occurred. Not only did their most prized cultural artifacts pass swiftly from the curbside to the supermarket, their vaunted new spirituality soon hardened into totalitarian religious cults; and the once-forbidden drugs for whose legitimizing they had called came to be more and more widely used—though, alas, for escapist "recreation" rather than to "alter consciousness."

By this time, moreover, I had exhausted what I had to say about *One Flew Over the Cuckoo's Nest* and other youth best-sellers of the sixties, and instead found myself turning to such favorite books of earlier generations as *Gone With the Wind* and *Uncle Tom's Cabin*. Though these had survived all the intervening changes of taste and lifestyle and, to tell the truth, long fascinated me, I had hitherto felt obliged to dismiss them as hopelessly "lowbrow." To be sure, I still also discussed works that had made it into the canon, including those Jewish American novels whose improbable triumph in the WASP world has always intrigued me. But typically I have done so from the viewpoint of a presumptuous outsider.

Introduction

Ever since the mid-seventies, I have found myself more and more often lecturing and writing not only on literature proper, high or low, but on bioethics, with whose very name I was not familiar until that very point. Throughout my career as a critic, I have been obsessed with the image of the Stranger, the Outsider, but chiefly as it is embodied in fictional portrayals of the ethnic Other. I have concentrated, that is to say, on the myths of the Negro, the Jew, and the Indian in novels and poems written by—and primarily for—WASP Americans. More recently, however, it occurred to me that for all of us able to think of ourselves as "normal," there is a more ultimate Other. That is, of course, the Freak, the Monster, the congenital malformation; a fellow-human born too large or too small, with too many or too few limbs, hair in the wrong places or ambiguous sexual organs. Such anomalous creatures have long been displayed at fairs and circuses, extorting shudders of repulsion and delight from a wider audience than those who experience them in response to dense and difficult works like *Moby Dick* or *Light in August*.

It was surely my sense that by turning to this subject I could reach a similar audience, which explained my otherwise inexplicable answer to a self-styled literary entrepreneur who happened to call me out of the blue. If I agreed to write a book on witchcraft, he began by assuring me, he could easily sell it to a major trade publisher and it would become a best-seller. Though I had indeed been obsessed by that queasy subject during my adolescence, I had long since lost all interest and so I declined. Was there any other subject with a similar popular appeal, he asked then, which I might be willing to treat? And without quite knowing why, I found myself answering, "Freaks." Moreover, before I had time to change my mind, I discovered that I had already scribbled down a couple of pages of notes for a book I was still not sure I would ever really write; on the basis of which (to my astonishment), he sold it to Simon and Schuster, who eventually peddled more copies of it than any work of mine had ever sold.

Actually completing it, however, was not so easy: not only did my uncustomary project take me into new areas of research, it led me into dark areas of my psyche which I had hitherto entered only in my most troubled dreams. Nevertheless, when I was done, it turned out that I had at long last broken through to the majority audience. I had been able to do so (it slowly dawned on me) without abandoning my lifelong exploration of the myths in which we come to terms with the ultimate mysteries of Love and Death, the Self and the Other.

But because this time I had dealt with those myths not just as they are figured forth in canonical literature and the art displayed in museums, but in sideshows, comic books, and pop music, I had, as it were, become visible to new eyes, audible to new ears. To begin with, *Freaks* was reviewed not only in respectable literary journals like the *New York Times Book Review* and the *New York Review of Books* but also in such less reputable periodicals as the *New York Daily News*, *Penthouse*, *Hustler*, and *High Times*. In addition, I found myself invited to appear as a guest on the talk show circuit; ineptly quizzed on the *Today Show*, the *Tomorrow Show*, the *Phil Donahue Show*, plus a slew of others on radio and TV.

Though the hosts of none of them had actually read my book, and some did not even properly remember my name, they all apparently felt obliged to display my face and book jacket on the screen as a kind of tribute paid by the acolytes of Pop Culture to the apostles of High Art; or perhaps, rather, an acknowledgment of the fact that I had gone part way toward closing the gap between the two cultures. After all, I had for the first time in my writing life produced a copiously illustrated volume: thus providing in effect, side by side with the Gutenberg text an iconic one, available to the majority audience which does not read print with ease and pleasure.

Some weeks after publication, in fact, I received a letter from a librarian in Philadelphia about a group of eight- or ten-year-old boys, who kept returning to gaze with horror and delight at the pictures which she displayed serially by flipping each day a different page of my book. For a while, therefore, I dared hope that it might even in the end be totally metamorphosed into post-print form—be turned, that is to say, into film. A movie of it was actually proposed and begun, in fact, but was abandoned after some preliminary shots; so I had to be content with appearing—side by side with a dwarf—in someone else's feature-length film. That strange by-product of my exposure on talk shows is, however, another story for another day.

For better or for worse, I had crossed the divide which separates the academy from Show Biz; and though some regarded that crossing as an abject capitulation to the marketplace, others recognized it as an attempt to break through disciplinary boundaries. For that reason, in the months after the appearance of *Freaks*, I not only appeared on the talk shows but also found myself addressing, in the flesh, people outside my field: psychologists, sociologists, social workers, and especially medical professionals. The latter seemed especially pleased to find a "humanist" willing to meet with them on the common ground of bioethics.

Not that all of them agreed with what I had to say on that contentious subject. Some of them, indeed, invited me only to chastise me as an intruder and set me right. But even they seemed glad to be able for once to disagree with someone like me face to face, rather than shouting insults back and forth—each of us safe in his departmental enclave.

In any case, I have continued talking over the past fifteen or twenty years to whoever will listen about gerontology, child abuse, euthanasia, cosmetic surgery, and organ transplants, as well as the images of doctors and nurses in literature and the popular arts. It should have been no surprise then (though I must confess I was a little astonished) to discover that the chief topic of this second collection of my more recent essays has turned out to be bioethics. After all, how could it not have in a world where the hospital has become a major institution, health care a universal concern; even as the moral implications of medical procedures bring demonstrators into the streets and make headlines in our daily newspapers.

Moreover, I myself (as some of these essays should make palpably clear) have reached an age at which my failing flesh reminds me at every moment that the ultimate questions about morality, normality, and identity are ones which, though we cannot finally answer them, whatever our area of expertise, it is incumbent on us, for the sake of our common humanity, to keep on asking.

LESLIE A. FIEDLER
Buffalo, New York

TYRANNY OF THE NORMAL

The Rebirth of God and the Death of Man

꧁

IT HAS, I ASSUME, become clear at this point to almost everyone that the successful Cultural Revolution we observed in the sixties and seventies—here in the United States at least, and perhaps generally in the Western World—the emergence of what has been called variously the "Counter Culture," or "Consciousness III," or "The New Mutants," or the "Present Future" has been in large part, even essentially, a *Religious Revival:* the unforeseen, unsung, and often quite misunderstood beginning of a New Age of Faith. The prophets of that Cultural Revolution, whether candid secularists like Wilhelm Reich and Herbert Marcuse or crypto-Thomists like Marshall MacLuhan, have, for reasons of their own, not emphasized this aspect of the movement they helped to create. And warmhearted but superficial analysts and apologists after the fact like Charles Reich or Theodore Roszak have obscured the religious dimensions of the Counter Culture (along with much else) because of their commitment to chic journalistic vocabularies intended to sell rather than describe what must be made at all costs to sound Brand New.

To be sure, one French opposite number of such apologists, Edgar Morin, declared his adherence to the New Movement with the phrase: "I am joining the Children's Crusade!" But in context (M. Morin is a sociologist and ex-Communist, or rather, I suppose, meta-Communist) this sounded like a mere metaphor—demanding immediate translation into more secular terms. Looking backward, however, it is possible to see (almost impossible to miss) what was, while it was happening, too obvious to be perceived: the fact that the recent Cultural Revolution has nurtured and, in a certain sense, *established* a dedicated minority felt by the larger society to be somehow representative, exemplary—even "sacred." It is further evident that the values of that minority, as embodied in a lifestyle celebrated or deplored daily (it amounts to much the same thing) by the popular press, are much like those traditionally associated with earlier exemplary minorities: lay clergy and cloistered religious, isolated hermits and utopian religious communities, sponsored or somewhat reluctantly endorsed by the established Churches.

I do not intend to discuss here the lifestyle in which these values are embodied, though certain aspects of this, too, provide obvious analogies into religious practices of the past. The actual garb of the New Communicants, for instance, these robes and sandals so appropriate to the pilgrimages in which they habitually engage, seem to me to be superficial and symptomatic rather than essential, as does the show of poverty which characterizes their way of life. Their pilgrimages may be merely a new form of bourgeois tourism or even of American cultural imperialism while their much-vaunted poverty is, perhaps, more aptly described as conspicuous under-consumption. It is, therefore, at a deeper level that I propose to begin, by examining their value system, at the center of which is the conviction that, after all, the contemplative life may be preferable to the active life. But, of course, to choose Rachel over Leah at this late date, the second wife of Jacob over his first, constitutes a radical rejection of the position defended against Catholic monasticism by an earlier Cultural Revolution launched by the Protestant churches: a position notoriously exploited by the secular heirs of Protestantism, the present Masters of our World, Capitalist and Communist alike.

From this major premise follow the corollaries that salvation rather than success is man's proper goal, and that, therefore, one must begin by rejecting goods in favor of the Good or even social welfare and learn eventually to prefer being good to being well—a shocking anti-psychiatric position. Furthermore, once contemplation is valued more highly than action, Vision rather than understanding is proposed as the proper end of man's inner life, the life of the mind. Oddly enough, I first became aware of this revolutionary shift in values in the classroom, where I teach from time to time courses on Dante, having done so, in fact, over the past three decades. During the first two of these decades, I was vexed by the sense of having to explain a radically alien point of view to my students before they could have any notion of what the poetry of the *Divine Comedy* was really about. But since 1960, there has been no need to spell out for students what "Vision" once meant to certain benighted believers since it is a category of experience to which they aspire even if they have not yet attained it. Still less is it necessary to expound for them the significance of the "Voyage" or, as it became more fashionable to call it at the time, the "Trip" through time to timelessness.

Never mind that the salvation sought by the New Religious is instant, here and now rather than at the end of days. Not they alone have become convinced that eternity does not lie beyond time but intersects it. Still less must we be put off by the fact that the New Celebrants seek Vision by the use of once forbidden drugs, revelation not just through fasting and prayer and spiritual exercise but by psycho-chemical means as well. All religions have employed intoxicants to initiate the entry into the Way—the grape, perfumes, music to aid in the trip toward ecstasy, where those means as well as everything else once prized and exploited will have become meaningless. After all, is not the ancient and holy practice of fasting itself a kind of negative psycho-chemistry?

We may *finally* be saved by that which comes out of the mouth rather than that which goes in, but all religions have initially concerned themselves with what is eaten as well as what is spoken: honoring not just the Word but Bread and Wine, as well as Dionysus and Ceres, the Gods poured out or consumed in honor of the other Gods. Besides, is there not implicit in the contemporary use of sacred drugs, of what is inadvertently sacred in the intend-edly profane pursuits of Science, a commendable desire to democ-ratize ecstasy, to make Mystical Vision no longer the privilege of a handful of adepts but of *everyone*. The New Religious are deter-mined to be no inert congregation rehearsing the words of dead Visionaries and half-mythological Saints, but a living church of actual Visionaries and Saints. This constitutes, perhaps, a pecu-liarly American dream, in its most virulent form even madder than our dream of universal higher education, this dream of universal *Ekstasis:* but, by the same token, it is even more beautiful—not least because it may be finally impossible, a Way to Idolatry more often than a Door to Perception.

Less noticed, perhaps, than the redemption of the Contempla-tive Life but almost as critically important, has been the Revolt against Romantic Love everywhere present within the ranks of the Cultural Revolution: the quite conscious attempt to liquidate the anti-religion or quasi-religion or burlesque religion of Love, which has possessed the Arts of Western Christendom and haunted the imaginations of all who have read its texts, or looked at its ikons, or listened to its quasi-holy songs since Courtly Love and vernac-ular poetry were born together at the end of the eleventh century in Provence. That essentially godless religion has come to seem to the New Communicants especially distasteful in its late Protestant-sentimental forms: that Angel-in-the-House tradition, in which the mock worship of women has been detached from adultery and linked to monogamous marriage and the bourgeois family.

Sometimes it is Sex—naked libido, unmythicized and polymor-phous perverse—which the New Believers oppose to Courtly or Romantic or Sentimental Love. Sometimes it is agape, Holy Love, Sweet Charity, a universal bond which, by making all men and women Brothers and Sisters, challenges the authenticity of those exclusive bonds which define us as Sons and Daughters, Mothers and Fathers, husbands and wives, and especially faithful and jealous lovers of other single humans. Sometimes, under the New Dispensation, undifferentiated libido and universal agape bled into one ambiguous impulse, capable of motivating the sort of sub-orgasmic orgies often called these days "Sensitivity Sessions" or "Encounter Groups" or, more pretentiously and equivocally, "Tribal Experiences."

A wide variety of sexual behavior is tolerated under the New Dispensation, ranging from the total sublimation of passion through multiple marriages to communities in which all are available in all possible ways to all: sex has become, like everything else, communal property. In no case, however, is exclusive heterosexual Love proposed as a means of Education and Civilization, a way of converting men and women, still moved by passion as dumbly and helplessly as beasts, into Ladies and Cavaliers, Courtiers distinguished by Gentle Hearts and the Intelligence of Love. And certainly the possibility has been preempted from the start of a compromise between *eros* and *agape*, the lust of the body and the longing of the soul, justified by the kind of Romantic Theology which begins with Dante's *Vita Nuova* and ends in the Anglican apologetics of Charles Williams, or the anti-Puritan Puritanism of D. H. Lawrence.

In addition to its attack on Work, Success, and Romantic Love, the New Religion is marked by an onslaught against certain conceptions of the central importance of Literature in the humanizing of man, conceptions which had remained basically unshaken (despite the rivalry of Science) ever since the Renaissance recovered from the Classical Past the notion of Culture as Secular Salvation for an educated elite. It is not, as Marshall MacLuhan, for instance, has argued, that the New Communicants, being children of an age dominated by the post-Gutenberg media, have ceased to read. MacLuhan is simply wrong in this regard. I have never visited an Agricultural Commune which does not possess some books—a slim collection of highly prized and carefully read volumes. But these must not be thought of as constituting in any traditional sense a "Library." No, in their function and use, they are more like the household books of some pious seventeenth century New England Puritan than the contents of nineteenth century study shelves stacked with critically approved "Great Books" or an early twentieth century parlor table loaded with the latest selections of the Book Clubs.

In place of the Puritan's Christian Bible, however, plus Milton and *Pilgrim's Progress*, one is likely to find a motley (but at last somehow standard) selection of some of the following: The *Tibetan Book of the Dead*, the *Whole Earth Catalogue*, and the *I Ching*; along with all three well-worn volumes of J. R. R. Tolkien's *Rings* trilogy, plus a Macrobiotic Cookbook, Kurt Vonnegut's *Cat's Cradle* or *Slaughterhouse Five*, Castañeda's *The Teachings of Don Juan*, a couple of Hermann Hesse novels, and a complete file of the latest Stan Lee comic books. And, as I had almost forgotten, there would also be some pornography: a "Head Comic" by R. Crumb, or a more grossly sadomasochistic one by S. Clay Wilson, or perhaps, *The Kama Sutra*.

The point is not merely that the Scripture of various alien cultures have been given equal—or even superior—status with the Holy Book of Christianity, but that *any books which are read at all are read as Scripture,* which is to say, not for information or "cultural enrichment" much less to pass an idle hour but as Guides to Salvation, and that even masturbatory fantasies are thus canonized. It does not matter, certainly, what the author of any particular text, chosen by some mysterious process associated with the marketplace and the mode, may have thought he was writing or why.

He may, like Robert Heinlein, for instance, when he corrected the last galleys of *A Stranger in a Strange Land,* have considered that he was producing just one more in a long line of Science Fiction novels intended to provide entertainment and make a quick buck. After all, at that point Heinlein was already a long-established and well-rewarded hack. But he could not stay the process which kidnapped his work for "sacred" ends, extracting from it a new "holy" verb ("to grok") and supplying the initial inspiration, as well as a passage or two for Charlie Manson's syncretic Black Ritual. And it does no good to protest later, as Heinlein has, along with the master of porno-sci-fi, Philip Jose Farmer, whose *The Lovers* apparently inspired him, that that is not what he meant at all. That *is* what they both meant *in context.*

Furthermore, it is neither accidental nor irrelevant that Heinlein's book comes from the area of Popular rather than High culture, the world of joyous junk rather than that of solemn art: for the new religion is essentially Pop. Pop Science is also raided in the endless search for a Pop Scriptures—as in the case of Ohsawa's various works on Dianetics. Or perhaps one should rather describe the texts of the founder of Macrobiotics as Pop Science plus Pop Theology: a little vulgarized Zen Buddhism, mingled with some Pop Reflections on Yin and Yang, plus some practical admonitions at the level of the Home Medical Advisor on how to cure gonorrhea and avoid cancer by learning to eschew milk. It does not matter that none of this makes rational sense. What does matter is precisely that it does not make such sense, thus providing occasions for true acts of faith. "I believe because it is absurd," the naive believer has always cried, scandalizing the more sophisticated who had placed their faith in the rational.

Certainly, the skeptical have not given pause to any devotee, however anemic and wasted, nor disturbed his resolution to go ten days on "straight grains" in quest of health more spiritual than physical. Mere medical statistics seem as irrelevant to such a believer as they had earlier to the followers of Wilhelm Reich who crouched naked in their "Orgone Accumulators" in quest of an orgasm pure enough to inhibit cancer. Nor does the sober comment of academic psychiatrists turn anyone away from the palpable "hoax" of Scientology: creation of L. Ron Hubbard, who was himself a hack-writer of Science Fiction before he decided to peddle his fantasies as fact—thus becoming the Founder of a New Faith, in whose name he has grown as rich as any Robber Baron or Park Avenue "shrink." But, of course, being a guru rather than a businessman or doctor or ordained clergyman, he finds it possible to remain immune to self-doubt or guilt. In an age of Underground Faith, the underground faithful rejoice especially in those leaders the established call "charlatans," in those who *are,* by established standards, charlatans in fact: from Hubbard and Leary and Manson to Wilhelm Reich.

But it is not charlatanism alone that moves the faithful. What are we to make, for instance, of the vogue of the Whole Earth Catalogue, the product not of showmen and hucksters, but of modest believers rather than arrogant Shamans, yet also a Pop, i.e., a commercial success? Is it not also a Bible for yet another Sect created in a time of Pop Science; and does it not reflect the teaching of yet another Science Fiction writer who has chosen life over art as his preferred medium: that odd blend of technocrat, guru and nut inventor, R. Buckminster Fuller? To be sure, his doctrine has been oddly transformed by being translated from the Urban centers he loves to the New Mexico countryside by younger men, less sure than he that technology can solve the problems it has created by becoming super-technology. It is a kind of sub-technology, which the editors of the *Whole Earth Catalogue* prefer, a minimal technology, a technology of do-it-yourself. But they share his faith, his Religion of Gadgetry; and in 1972, their technocrats Bible was given, scandalizing some and gratifying others, a National Book Award.

The judges who bestowed that award were merely attempting to certify as "literature" a somewhat pretentious collection of ads for goods still considered "kosher" in a time of conspicuous underconsumption. But the early admirers of the *Whole Earth Catalogue* had already canonized it as "Scripture." So that even before the National Book Award, it had made its way on to the shelves of readers who would never use any of the products it advertised—having no desire to build super-geodesic domes or assemble prefabricated Indian teepees, but merely to read or own a Holy Text.

How different has been the fate of the *Sears Roebuck Catalogue,* its predecessor and prototype, which only came to be esteemed and preserved when it had grown obsolete enough to the advanced to seem proper "camp." To be sure, the *Sears Roebuck Catalogue* evoked no holy names like that of Buckminster Fuller, no sacred theory like his. But this is not the real point; for in the declining twentieth century, what is most debased, most despised, most utterly vulgarized in the realm of para-literature, i.e., advertising, is all the more prized, so long as it can be used for presumed "sacred" ends: turning on, returning to nature, dropping out, avoiding pollution, ripping off the Establishment. It has, in fact, always been true in the case of Pop Religions, in America at least—Christian Science, for example, and Mormonism—that the low literary value of New Scriptures has been taken as a warranty of their sincerity and truth.

And here, precisely, is where the habit of reading literature as Scripture so essential to the New Dispensation differs totally from the elitist "Culture Religion" whose great apostle was Matthew Arnold. For Arnold, what made literature, some literature, Scripture, or rather a replacement for Scripture in an age of declining faith and The Death of God, was its excellence as literature, and its consequent critical immortality. On the other hand, what makes literature, some literature, available as Scripture in an Age of the Revival of Faith and the rebirth of the Gods is its doctrinal content, in the light of which the very nature of literary excellence, in aesthetic or formalist terms, becomes not merely irrelevant, but offensive as well. Once more, it is not that literary excellence is felt as totally inimical to relevance or truth, for some of the canonical texts of the New Dispensation are worthy enough for formalist standards: Tolkien, for example, or Hesse, or Kurt Vonnegut. And yet even these contain a redeeming element of *schlock* or *schmaltz,* or at least *Kitsch.*

Beyond the rejection of the Puritan Ethos and Love and Literature, there resides at the heart of the current Religious revival a fourth rejection, not less noticed, perhaps, but certainly less clearly understood than any of the others; and yet without coming to terms with it, we cannot fully comprehend the meaning of the Cultural Revolution. This is the Rejection of the City, a flight from urban to rural, which seems at first glance merely a reaction (comprehensible enough, and even sympathetic) from the unseemly sprawl, the congestion and pollution, the antihuman pace and the aggravated offense against nature apparently inseparable from urban civilization. But the New Mutants in their agricultural communes cannot be understood merely as the last heirs of a tradition of revulsion which, over the past two or three centuries, has driven increasing numbers of sensitive souls to abandon the centers of large cities and to create first the Romantic Suburb, then the Bourgeois Suburb, and finally, Exurbia: all bound still to the urban core by trains and buses and private cars, a network of two-way roads leading back and forth from markets and jobs and theaters at the center to gardens and bedrooms on the periphery. No, the agricultural commune is no ultimate exurb disguised as a rural slum, nor even a cross between Exurbia and Bohemia. It is an outward and visible manifestation of an inward and invisible rejection not just of the *metropolis* and *megalopolis* but of the *polis* itself: not just of New York and Berlin and Tokyo and London but of Rome and Athens, Florence and Urbino, Vicenza and Weimar, in favor of Green Belt and Bucks County.

There has been a deep ambivalence toward the city apparent at the heart of our culture ever since the city was reinvented sometime around the twelfth century. In Dante, for instance, innermost Hell, the heart of the Inferno, is thought of as a "sorrowful city," *la città dolente*: but in the ultimate Empyrean, he remembers the Holy City, stronghold of Empire and Papacy. And we are, therefore, not surprised when he draws on his tourist's memories of Rome for the setting of his final vision, portraying the Saints gathered together in an arena which is simultaneously a Rose and the Coliseum, the perfection of natural beauty and urban architecture. It is not the redeemed, the Heavenly City, which the New Religious dream but a world without cities—a world before or after cities, a world in which the Idea of the City has not yet been conceived or has been long forgotten. This is because Dante is already a Humanist, as the New Religious no longer are.

The idea of Man central to Humanism is inseparable from the Idea of the City: the notion of a complex community based on the division of labor, the centralization of specialized services plus a concentration of talent, a maximization of cultural interchange, as well as the storage and distribution of the most varied kinds of goods. The actualization of this Idea made possible the creation of theaters and supermarkets, libraries and museums, hospitals and cathedrals, courts of law and parliaments, and supereminently, the University, the center and shrine, as it were, of dialectics and of the conversion of *mythos* to *logos*, the Shrine of Humanism. The End of the City, the death of the *polis* means, therefore, the End of Man as we have defined him over the past two and a half millennia. I scarcely need remind you of the Aristotelian text which is a chief source of that definition. *Man is a political animal; outside the polis, he is a beast or a god.* Nor is it necessary to do more than mention the literary work which constitutes a kind of dramatic and still half-mythic prefiguration of that text, since it is a work which has preeminently possessed our imaginations over the past decade or so, becoming for us by all odds the favorite, the most living of all classic Greek dramas. I am referring, of course, to *The Bacchae* of Euripides, which renders with total clarity, though without simplification of the ambiguities involved, the crisis of the human which occurs when men grow weary of the institutions which have nurtured their humanity; or rather, perhaps, when those institutions rigidify to the point at which creative sublimation becomes deadly repression, and *logos* becomes madness both for those who remain behind in the dying city and those who abandon the *polis* in favor of the *thiasos*, the pack, the Dionysiac rout.

There is no other alternative; when we flee the City, we wake to find ourselves on Cithaeron, which is to say, in a world without order or tradition or law or distinction: the Dionysiac world, which it is possible to glorify by expurgation à la Nietzsche as a source of fertility and song (which it is), a place where madness has at least a sanctified function. But, as Euripides confessed long ago, it is also a world of ecstasy from which one awakens, inevitably, necessarily, to terror: the Mother discovering that the bloody head she holds in her hand is not that of some sacrificial beast, but of her Son who, refusing to sanctify madness in the name of the human, himself becomes simultaneously a beast and a God, though still somehow a mortal who must suffer and be destroyed.

But here precisely is the essence of the thiasic as opposed to political experience, of life in the pack as opposed to life in the city. For in the *thiasos*, all those distinctions are lost which made possible the play of dialectic and the reign of reason: between male and female, god and man, god and beast, drunkenness and sobriety, sanity and insanity, waking and sleeping, Yes and No. The realm of indistinction is, however, the realm of the metahuman: a realm we inhabit only in dreams—dreams in which, alas, we can no longer remain forever, like our prehuman ancestors, but from which we are doomed always to awake. This we tend to forget in the drunken roar of Dionysiac release, at the Demonstration, the Orgy, the Rock Festival, the child's Saturday matinee at the movies, the adult's Sunday afternoon in the football stadium, when speech yields to noise (one name of the terrible God of the Pack is Bromios, the Roarer). It is, of course, in this world, the world of noise, of static and anti-messages, of overloaded circuits and amplifiers turned up to full that the New Religious live by choice, and the rest of us, willy-nilly, assaulted by record players or radios or the jukebox, bullhorns, or the screaming of crowds.

Noise or silence—but not speech, dialogue, communication— are proper to the realm of the ineffable, the metapolitical, the divine. One pole of the possibilities inherent in the New Religions, the New Religiosity, is, then defined by the legend of Dionysus, as the adaptation of Euripides' play by Richard Schechner, *Dionysus in '69*, made clear—involving the audience itself, when it worked best, in the updated, naked Dionysiac rout it re-created in a theater that ceased to be a theater as the beholders became participants, followers of the Impostor God, the actor whose very act of imposture was proof of his Dionysiac claims. The God who was not a God but a neighborhood freak in a theater which was not a theater but unstructured space, displaying his sex before spectators who, if moved, knew they were not spectators but celebrants and victims who had paid to be so trifled with, so transformed: perhaps this was as close as we could come in our time to the true orgy, thiasic release. But maybe it was as close as anyone—after the building of cities, whether Thebes or New York—could *ever* come; emerging inevitably to other noises, other silences: the roar of the traffic which bears us home, the silence of our own house before we turn on the TV to watch the late, late show or alternatively, the blaring insistence of the music our children are listening to when we enter. "Turn it down," we are likely to yell, glad to have a noise level we can control—not off, but *down*, for we find total silence also an affront.

Not so those pledged to meditation, who pursue, through techniques adapted from Yoga—legs folded in the lotus position or pressed tight as they stand on their heads—what they learned to call (while Zen was fashionable) "the sound of one hand clapping." There is in our own Western tradition a myth of Silence equivalent to the Dionysiac Myth of Noise, which, I cannot help believing, is on the verge of moving once again to the center of our imagination. This is the Legend of the Holy Grail—that terrifying account of the destruction of a society based on chivalric valor and courtly love by the pursuit of what exists only outside of all communities, which is to say, Nowhere. The present age, which has also turned its back on traditional notions of heroism and romance in its pursuit of vision, should find this myth particularly sympathetic, yet there has been no contemporary adaptation of the Holy Grail story equivalent to Schechner's revision of *The Bacchae,* only children's stories and musical comedy versions of Arthurian story on the level of *Camelot*—or, more interestingly, infinite variations in search of a new classic form in Science Fiction, short or long.

In fiction and verse, however, the major attempts to reveal the relevance of the Grail symbol to a time of reviving Faith have been made by writers whose religion is nostalgic rather than prophetic and whose aesthetic stance belongs to a moment when Modernism had not yet yielded to the post-Modern: John Cooper Powys in the *Glastonbury Romance,* Charles Williams in *War in Heaven,* and especially Eliot in his incoherent *The Wasteland,* framed on the one side by Jessie L. Weston's scholarly study, *From Ritual to Romance,* and on the other by Bernard Malamud's *The Natural.* Yet there is scarcely anyone among the New Mutants who is unfamiliar, through one child's adaptation or another, with Malory's *Morte d'Arthur,* that melancholy account of the end of the Round Table, the death of Arthur, and the destruction of Lancelot and Guinevere by the pure Knight who comes from silence and disappears into silence, creating nothing, only laying waste the world. If *The Bacchae,* especially as interpreted by Richard Schechner, was appropriate to the mounting ecstasy of the sixties, the Legend of the Grail seems an oracular prophecy, awaiting an interpreter, of the desolation which has succeeded it at a moment when the Rock Festivals have passed into the hands of the commercial exploiters, when the legendary fraternity of the Beatles falls apart in squabbles over money or prestige, when Lenny Bruce and Janice Joplin are dead—and the most devout among us withdraw into silent meditation.

In the world of silence, as in the world of noise, worship is possible as well as ecstasy, but not theology. The New Communicants begin where Thomas Aquinas ended, crying of his own *Summa Theologica,* "It is all rubbish." They know from the start that theology belongs to the realm of *Wissenschaft*—an alternative way toward vision, perhaps, quite like though less sympathetic to them than the use of intoxicants and like the latter tending to become an occasion for Idolatry when considered an end rather than a means. And they sense somehow at this point that the Death-of-God Theology was the last theology of the West, since what it was talking about, what it foresaw, was its own death—the death of a method rather than its subject.

We live at a moment when the God of the Science of God is dead, so that the Science of Religion, invented in the eighteenth century, has become as unviable as the Religion of Science invented at the same time. We must not be misled in this regard by the growing popularity of university courses in "Theology," courses crowded these days with precisely the New Communicants we have been discussing. Their uses of such courses are eccentric, illegitimate in fact from any "scholarly" point of view, since they enter them in quest of ecstasy and entertainment, more material to be stored in the do-it-yourself kits for salvation that they will take with them when they leave the University for the desert, the classroom for the Commune. Instinctively, they know that they must translate an ancient symbolic language into Pop Mythology, like that elaborated in the Stan Lee New Apocalypse series of comic books, in which Christian eschatology has replaced Captain Marvel and the myth of the secular savior bred in the modern city. To recover that ancient language they raid even classes in Theology, "spoiling the Egyptians," as the old phrase has it.

It must not be thought, however, that they share the rationalist or rationalizing motives of their teachers. Indeed, they stand on its head the humane and scholarly tradition which begins with the Socratic slogan, "The unexamined life is not worth living" and comes to a climax in the Freudian tag—inspired by Part II of *Goethe's Faust*, itself inspired by the secular triumphs of Dutch land-reclamation: "Where *id* was *ego* shall be." The votaries of the noisiest of Gods and of the silence which follows his triumph have turned all that upside down—crying out in the rout (and minding not a bit if no one can really hear what they say): "Only the unexamined life is worth living" and "Where *ego* is, *id* shall return!" No wonder, then, that the New Religious reject utterly not merely those churches of the West which have become hopelessly genteel but any which have compromised with Humanism. Christian Humanism, Judaeo-Humanism, any attempt to reconcile reason and faith, ecstasy and dialectic: this is the Enemy. "Dehumanize yourselves," cry the New Antihumanists. "Dare be more than human or less."

That is why, when they do not create for themselves homemade Churches out of Popular Science, they turn either to the religions of the original inhabitants of our own continent or to those of the original Indians after whom they were named in error. The native American Church, that odd blend of Protestant fundamentalism and the ritualized consumption of peyote buttons, has been especially appealing, since it involves the use of hallucinogens and was blessed in the beginning by Timothy Leary. And what could be finally more sympathetic to the supermarket syncretism of our times than devotees who pray to Jesus, Mary, and Peyote? But the East Indians have proved even more so, proving once more that America is still the "Passage to India" Whitman called it. Not only Whitman was moved in the nineteenth century to turn east in search of a new scriptures but Emerson and Thoreau as well. Typically, however, the New Communicants resemble Whitman rather than Thoreau in that they tend to adapt rather than assimilate Indian religions, almost deliberately half understanding them. In the end, therefore, whatever those religions may have meant to their original believers, to the New Religious in our midst they represent essentially what is least familiar in their world, most alien to their own believing ancestors: a polar opposition to Aquinas or Maimonides.

Typically, they respond to such religions in their shabbiest, their most vulgar forms: if Zen Buddhism, as in the late fifties Zen was expounded by popularizers like Alan Watts. But it is more lumpen movements, like Krishna Consciousness, which they prefer, as anyone knows who has confronted on the street corners of the world in recent years those shaven-headed youths clashing cymbals and crying for alms. So also they seek out the sect that developed around Meher Baba, that most Pop of avatars, who looked like the late great comedian, Jerry Colonna, loved movies and cricket, and died ("dropped his body") without breaking his decades of silence as his followers had been long promised he would—a last vaudeville gag. If the mythology of Christianity has been accepted, it is notoriously closer to Billy Graham or even Billy Sunday than to Ellery Channing or Cotton Mather. Similarly, it is latter-day Chasidism which appeals to converts out of all the possible varieties of Judaism: to the followers of the Lubovitcher *Rebbe* recruiting with astonishing success among the longhairs, hippies, and freaks.

But this is by no means the nadir or the acme of the New Crusade which has led also to a revival of Satanism and Witchcraft, limited most often to simple theatrics and the cry (without consequence), "Evil be thou my good!" but occasionally eventuating in orgiastic Sabbaths and even (as the Manson affair made manifest) in ritual murder. Everywhere, however, the latest recrudescence of Black Magic has been essentially popular and democratic, sometimes downright shoddy and subliterate: a kind of Satanism for everyone—clearly distinguished from that elitist devil worship which appealed to an aristocratic few at the end of the last centur, and is memorialized in literary works intended for a highly educated audience, like Huysman's *Là-Bas* or the poems of William Butler Yeats.

The New Diabolism reflects, in this sense, the redemption, so characteristic of the movement, of everything which Science and respectable Religion had agreed in labeling "mere superstition": alchemy, astrology, fortune-telling, all that had long been relegated to certain charlatans on shabby back streets or the filler columns in the popular press and the *Farmer's Almanac*. It is precisely the disreputable, antirational aura of these subsciences or anti-sciences that moves the young in an age which prefers astrology to astronomy, alchemy to chemistry, magic to technology: an age in which, among the New Mutants at least, the question "What are you?" is typically answered not with "A student, a priest, a scientist," or even "A man" but with "A Pisces" or "A Scorpio." And each eventless day is likely to begin with a casting of the *I Ching* or shuffling the Tarot pack.

Moreover, this double revolt of visionary youth against rational religion and science is matched in some sense, perhaps essentially embodied, in the reappearance among them of certain "plagues" once nearly subdued by the combined efforts of laboratory researchers and medical technicians, plus a code of personal hygiene propagated first by primary school teachers, and then by the pseudo-Doctors in white coats on TV ads for toothpaste or sanitary napkins. There is something repulsive to anyone committed to living in his physical body and remaining faithful to his animal inheritance in the compulsive American drive (most recently and hysterically joined by upwardly mobile Blacks) to scrub, cleanse, and deodorize oneself out of all semblance of physical humanity. Only when touring the remotest corners of the "backward" world, or lost in the midst of combat, or taken by chance or conscience into the houses of the hopeless poor does the modern Western bourgeois catch a whiff of man's ancient smell, the true odor of mortality.

The invention of the flush toilet, perhaps, began it all—concealing from him his own wastes and precipitating an early ecological crisis, as the residue of what we had eaten and digested no longer fertilized what was to feed us next. This was succeeded by the cosmeticizing and deodorizing of the dead, as a whole culture reinvented mummification in an effort to hide from sight the inevitability of death and decay. And what has finally followed everyone knows who watches daytime television, in which the truly sacred dramas (interspersed by secular ones, called significantly "Soap Operas" or just "Soaps") are Commercials dedicated to products guaranteed to remove mouth odor, body odor, kitchen odor, toilet odors, the natural smell of the genitals themselves: the basic scent of our dying bodies, without an awareness of which no religion seems necessary or possible.

No wonder the New Communicants have turned from this travesty-transformation of apocalyptic expectation onto therapeutic hygiene, this attempt to create a redeemed and purified body Here and Now—along with the implicit Credo that uncleanliness is not merely next to godliness but is all the godliness we need. No wonder they flee hot water and find pseudo-scientific reasons for eschewing soap, insisting that what in one sense cleans, in another, deeper sense pollutes. No wonder they leave behind "sanitary plumbing" and shit on the beaches and wooded hillsides of our own wilderness areas or whatever remote land they reach in their ceaseless pilgrimages, which seem not so much voyages to Holy Places as flights from an unholy one: from the tiled bathroom with its locked door and stock of required reading.

More, however, is involved than the rejection of commercialized hygiene. The true, the ultimate enemy is modern medicine itself, most despised of the anti-magical sciences, most distrusted of the secular technologies. It is, in part, *institutionalized* medicine which the New Communicants fear, associating it, on the one hand, with that soulless totalitarian institution, the Hospital, especially its psychiatric wards, where ecstasy is labeled "madness," and "sanity" is enforced with shock treatments and lobotomies. On the other hand, they cannot separate it from the "Doctor," that $50,000-a-year AMA member, bad enough in reality and worse in their paranoic vision of him as a racist, sexist exploiter of his patients—dedicated to supporting "unjust" wars while resisting "just" causes like socialized medicine, free access to drugs, euthanasia, and legalized abortion.

For a while, the New Communicants opposed to that bogeyman certain "good" doctors of their own, most notably the famous "Dr. Hippocrates," whose columns of irreverent and fashionable hip advice appeared in the underground press. But Dr. Hippocrates then passed from favor for pointing out, in an access of responsibility, the danger to life itself of the famous ten-days "straight-grain" regime sponsored by the Macrobiotic Faith. It is quackery they prefer, flagrant antiscience as preached by Ohsawa himself, or L. Ron Hubbard or Wilhelm Reich (anyone who seems more Medicine Man than professional practitioner).To be sure, some medical practices seem acceptable to the New Religious, especially if they are sponsored by regimes on the Left: acupuncture, for instance, which was officially blessed by Mao-Tse-Tung. But perhaps even its appeal is based not so much on its acceptance in Communist China as on its rejection by official circles in the United States; its aura of unredeemable disputability. After all, it was first advertised on the American Scene not in some Maoist journal but in the pornographic pop novel, *Candy*.

Basically, however, there has been a movement away from all medical treatment, public as well as private, in favor of do-it-yourself techniques ranging from therapeutic diets to the use of hand-held vacuum devices for abortions. Birth control has posed, in fact, a special problem, since contraceptive pills and the "loop" represent final achievements of the hated medical technology and its marketplace ethos. Chastity and homosexuality seem more truly religious methods of population control, being more easily adapted to antitechnological myths: yet despite some talk of sexual abstinence and of *coitus riservatus* as practiced in certain Tantrist sects or among the Yogin, and the popularity in the Feminist movement of Lesbian Unions, the major drift of the New Religious has been toward pansexuality and the Orgy—solutions which in a real sense presuppose modern contraception.

It is, in any case, infestation and disease which have tended to occupy the center of the rekindled religious imagination rather than purity or continence; so that even though no major sect has raised the cry, "Sickness is preferable to health" (except in the limited area of mental health), many new Communicants act *as if* this were an essential article of their faith. And their rejection of established modes of prevention and treatment have eventuated in the return to the universities and the bourgeois suburbs of certain minor nuisances, once believed gone forever, like head lice and crab lice, as well as major diseases like gonorrhea and syphilis and infectious hepatitis. But hepatitis can be checked by careful sterilization of hypodermic needles (the chief source of its spread), and the common venereal diseases were on the point of disappearing in the decade after World War II, which had seen the development of ever more powerful antibiotics. Indeed, there is no "rational" explanation for their failure to become as obsolete as diphtheria and smallpox, no emergence of an especially virulent strain of gonococci or spirochetes (as is sometimes believed) immune to these new "wonder drugs." No, what is involved is simply a refusal to be diagnosed or, once diagnosed, to follow prescribed treatments: a refusal based on a quite conscious contempt for science and a half-conscious longing for disease as some ultimate symbol of liberation.

It is no surprise that the highest incidence of venereal disease have occurred precisely in the holy places of the New Religious: the Haight-Ashbury, for example, and the agricultural communes, where a few instances of Plague have also been reported. The very universal love and emancipated sexuality which characterize the New Faiths at their best become a means of mutual infection and reinfection: while dirty needles used to inject ecstasy-producing drugs lead to stupor and coma and total collapse, as released bile invades the bloodstreams of the devout.

It is possible, to be sure, to put all of this in historical context, reminding ourselves that all Crusades, i.e., resurgences of religious faith leading to the breaking of old cultural boundaries, have resulted in similar outbreaks of pestilence. We can think, for instance, of how the late Medieval wars against Islam, presumably intended to repossess the Holy Land, brought back into Europe leprosy; or how the Discovery of America conducted by one who called himself the "Christ-bearing Dove" and sailed on a ship named after the Blessed Virgin, resulted in the first major outbreak of syphilis in the western world. To be sure, the Medieval Crusades were not fought solely, or perhaps even chiefly, to redeem Christian shrines; nor were the voyages of exploration primarily intended, as Roman Catholic apologists argued, to find a new source of souls as replacements for those lost to the Protestant Revolt. And one can read the body-wasting diseases that resulted as outward and visible signs of the impure motives, political and commercial, which underlay and undercut their avowed ends.

But perhaps it is better to understand such "plagues" as physical manifestations of profounder psychic events: the culture shocks resulting from an encounter with other societies based on differing concepts of the human and divine, as well as rival religions created to sanction such concepts. The current Cultural Revolution represents a movement in inner space rather than outer, a psychological rather than a geographical journey; but it, too, has resulted in an encounter with an alien type of man, the Barbarian inside our old humanist selves. How appropriate, then, seems the reinvention of syphilis, a "disease" associated (quite like the natural hallucinogenic drugs) with the American Indian, in whom the New Mutants have found a model for their alternative lifestyle. No new Gods without new diseases seems to be the lesson of history; no resurgence of faith without new mortifications of the flesh at the unconscious or psychosomatic level, as well as on levels where reason and consciousness fully function. But this means, in the end, new definitions of "sickness" and "health."

We have known all along that when Dionysus comes he brings affliction to the spirit, "madness" in terms of the society he scourges. Why is it more difficult to accept the fact that he occasions afflictions of the flesh as well, "sickness" in the language of the world he teaches us to deny. And the same is surely true of the *deus absconditus* of the Grail Legend, that God who, unlike the

Christian God, neither begets a Savior on the Jewish mother (the father of Galahad is Lancelot, which is to say, depraved and passionate man) nor reveals himself. In the end, the insufferably pure hero disappears from us, leaving the world a little worse than when he entered, since woman is bereft of her adulterous champion and the realm of its betrayed king. Even the symbols the Grail Knight *has* seen are symbols of infertility: Cup and Dish, Lance and Sword—the receptacles for Wine and Bread and the phallic weapons, one broken, one bleeding, eternally sundered from the female vessels. There is no Bible which follows such a revelation, only an unfinished, unfinishable popular poem by a hundred authors, and the pips on the Tarot deck, used first to tell fortunes and at last only to amuse the bored. How fitting that this myth survive among us chiefly in children's books and musical comedies, and finally in the literary texts (even Eliot's *Wasteland*) read only by scholars.

But he is a real God, though his name is never spoken, this God whose story begins in silence and failure only to end in silence and success. His unspoken name, I suppose, is death. But he is nonetheless quite as genuine, as authentic as the other God whose names are many and cried aloud: Bacchus, Baccheus, Iacchos, Bassareus, Bromios, Evios, Sabazios, Zagreus, Thyoneus, Lenaios, Eleotheos, the Imposter, the Intoxicator, the Twice Born, the Phallus, the Ox, the Voice, the Pine Tree, Noise and Madness. When god is dead, a Christian theologian predicted not so long ago, the Gods will be reborn: or, to change the metaphor, once the Guardian at the Twin Gates of Dream, Ivory, and Horn, has been removed, the undying Gods will reappear. And why, then, would we hesitate to hail those who have opened the unguarded Gate dancing at the head of a procession whose end no one can see and shouting prophecies too loud to be heard? What if they scratch themselves, head and crotch, as they come; or even if the embrace they offer threatens infection and pain and death itself?

Not only have they performed the Hermetic function, turning

themselves into *theopompoi*, heralds of the Gods. They have already begun to create a *cultus* appropriate to those Gods, as well as institutions to promulgate their faith and to preserve it in a hostile or indifferent world: the Demonstration, the Rock Festival, the Encounter Group. These variations on the Orgy (more like the American Revival Meeting, perhaps, than remoter Greek models), sublimated, half-sublimated, or totally desublimated, constitute their missionary institutions. And no vulgarization or commercialization can impugn them; for they are, by definition, vulgar and commercial, immune to "humanization" or polite piety. Nor does an eruption of violence, even murder itself, such as "marred" the Rolling Stones orgiastic moment at Altamont, undercut their effectiveness. Like the stoned-out kids or the exhibitionist publicly masturbating on flagpoles at Woodstock, Mick Jagger invoking death for unknown others is part of the meaning of it all: ugly, dark, dangerous, ambiguously suspended between *eros* and *thanatos* like the god himself.

Finally, however, it is their preservative institutions which seem the most vital and significant achievement of the New Age of Faiths: the asylums or refuges established for those already sanctified or in search of sanctity (or only tired and hungry and spaced out) in certain green interstices of our industrialized world: the Agricultural Communes. They have been sufficiently portrayed, in their bewildering variety and final unity, at all levels of scholarship and journalism; and the sense of their living reality has been rendered in fiction and verse as well as in film. There seems, therefore, little point in rehearsing either their virtues (the sense of community and peace, the possibility of nonmedical therapy) or their faults (the equivocal role of the gurus who lead them, their instability, the hostility they engender in their neighbors). It is now clear that they are viable and that they will persist for better or worse, as we still say, in a world where few agree on the meaning of better or worse. But it is equally clear that they will persist in a larger world that will, by and large, not follow their example but continue to emulate commercial, competitive, and even violent social models.

Yet, like the monasteries of the Middle Ages, they have already altered the meaning of everything done around them, even in contempt of all they represent. Our Era can, in fact, be described as a Religious one not because all, or indeed most of us, live by a code which honors Contemplation and Vision, but because a few men and women, chiefly but not exclusively young, are laying up in isolation a kind of spiritual capital for us all by living a life that many outside of their retreats are even now beginning to yearn for, or wish they yearned for, or wish they wished they yearned for. Certainly, most of us already envy them their presumed indolence, their boasted sexual freedom, their unashamed nakedness, and their apparent deliverance from urban ennui. There is, consequently, little doubt in my mind that in the near future our presiding form of hypocrisy will be the rhetorical tribute our vice pays to their virtue.

At that point, the analogy will be complete; and we will have as much right to call ourselves Dionysiacs or Anabaptists or orgiasts or ecstatic polytheists as the men of the Middle Ages had to call themselves Christians, despite their wars and uncharity and daily desecration of the their official faith. For just as those would-be Christians endured or tolerated, sometimes even supported certain cloistered religious who *lived* the faith they could not really abide, so we are learning to endure or tolerate, even directly or by indirection to support the hippies and freaks who are ushering in a New Dispensation we fear.

Yet how can we bring ourselves to applaud without reservation a group of believers who offer us a kind of salvation, to be sure, a way out of the secular trap in which we have been struggling, but who are themselves ridden by superstition, racked by diseases spread in the very act of love, dedicated to subverting sweet reason through the use of psychedelic drugs and the worship of madness, committed to orgiastic sex and doctrinaire sterility, pursuing ecstasy even when it debauches in murder, denying finally the very ideal of the human in whose name we have dubbed our species *Homo sapiens?* If this is the price of religious renewal, who would not choose even the "quiet desperation" of Death-of-God Capitalism or Communism, both committed, in theory at least, to maximizing our earthly goods, minimizing suffering and pain, extending life, and organizing the relations of the sexes in some rational and stable way.

Even if we stand in need of salvation rather than success or social welfare (as the equal though quite different anguish of rich and poor, male and female, Black and White, old and young among us suggests we do), surely we must look for that salvation to some other quarter. And yet I myself have been moved to the very verge of ecstasy, over the lintel of joy in precisely such religious communities as I have been describing; so that finally I can, *must* cast a balance in the most personal of terms.

Let me cite two instances. When my first grandson was born some four years ago, I found that I wanted him to be circumcised like all of his male ancestors for three thousand years; but not medically, therapeutically only and not certainly in the mumbled ritual of a tongue and faith no longer comprehensible to most of those who would be present. I decided, therefore, that I would adapt the ancient formulae to my own sense of the times, presiding, though leaving the actual cutting of the foreskin to a doctor from some church-sponsored hospital in New Mexico, Baptist or Methodist, I am no longer sure. The doctor, however, though a proper white-coated technologist, too emancipated certainly to suck a drop of blood from the child's penis like a traditional *moel,* was at least a Jew. Not so, the young congregation that assembled from a nearby commune called the Domes. They were, in overwhelming majority, goyim, though bearded and sandaled and robed quite like my own ultimate forebears: living great-grandparents, as it were, a living past somehow grown younger than I. But is that not the way one remembers the grandparents of his grandparents, as he himself grows older in the trap of time which they have long since escaped?

There is one point in the ancient ceremony when the Celebrant says to the child, who actually bleeds in full view of all, his pain subdued by his first sip of wine, *"I say unto you, 'In your blood live!' Yea, I say unto you, 'In your blood live!' "* And the young man who stood behind me, blond-bearded and blue-eyed, his Gentile head half a foot above my own, responded, "Heavy trip, man!" and fainted. It was a response written in no prayerbook, but it was the right response. Because for once, for the first time in my fifty years of life, a *Brith,* a commemoration of our ancient Covenant with the God we thought dead was really *happening!* Before the ceremony was over, two other people had gone down, because (I was suddenly aware) they had learned again the meaning of Sacrifice and the required shedding of blood, beyond all rational talk of "symbolic wounds" or liberal horror at the persistence of cruel and archaic rites. Afterwards, we drank and danced, like my own Chasidic ancestors, for how many hours I cannot say, since we were out of time. And, at last, intoxicated and worn out, we slept, waking to joy with the next day. God knows (some reborn god) precisely what it was in me that danced and slept and waked and rejoiced: the undying child, perhaps, or the unredeemed savage, the unrecorded Polish rapist, or the half-remembered wonder-*rebbe* who healed the lame and raised the dead—maybe all of them, all of me except my customary professorial self, though, I suppose, that too. And why not?

So I danced again (I who cold sober never dance, know when I am cold sober that, whatever I remember, I really never *have,* except maybe in my head), as I had actually danced at Purim services a year ago, my second son by my side. Purim is an odd holiday in the Jewish year to begin with, a mad occasion of masking and carnival release in honor of a woman: a Jewish girl, presumably, who began by dancing naked before a Pagan King, then married him, and ended saving her people from the destruction plotted by that King's evil prime minister. But Esther is finally no Jewish girl at all, her name a Hebrew variant of Ishtar-Ashtoreth-Astarte, just as the name of her presumed uncle, Mordecai, is another form of Marduk. She is, in short, the great Goddess herself smuggled into its imaginary history by the most patriarchal of faiths. But never mind. Jews have danced and sung in drunken joy life to her and death to her enemy, Haman (it is taught that on Purim a good Jew must get so drunk that he cannot tell Haman from Mordecai), for centuries now. And what better place to continue that tradition than in the converted clam bar which serves as a synagogue for that same Chasidic sect which cries on the campuses, "LSD means *lets start davaning*." And *davan* we did, swaying and chanting in prayer, with a congregation consisting chiefly of half-converted longhairs and freaks, though a few old men as well, and a handful of orthodox in their long black coats.

My son and I are joined in memory and love always, but seldom in pious practice. He is a food freak, a refugee from cities—who, while I am pounding my typewriter or opening my mail, will be crouched on the grass in lotus position or standing on his head bolt upright and stark naked in his lonely room. But for once we moved together in a common living present, joined by a magic to which, momentarily at least, we both subscribed. And our dead ancestors danced with us, at home with the bearded kids, high perhaps on grass, and the *chasidim*, a little drunk surely on rye whiskey. We had for that little while resurrected the dead, our own dead, given life to those who gave us the gift of life, and to the Father of us all, whose name we still did not say even when we knew he was dead. But his names are many, after all, since he is Many as well as One, is reborn as One when he dies as Many, twice reborn as Many when he dies as One: Jehovah and Elohim, Dionysus and Bacchus, or, alternatively, Astarte and Leukothea, Ishtar and Aphrodite and Cybele, it makes no difference. The women, young girls chiefly, were confined to the back of the synagogue, behind a screen, but somehow they knew. Together we had created the gods who created our humanity, male and female created we them. A minute later, of course, we were awake, sundered from each other, the past and those gods. But that, too, didn't, doesn't matter; couldn't, as the colloquial phrase has it, matter less.

And knowing this, I know what I must answer when the Priests and Professors, to whose world I return from the *Brith* and the exclam-bar, cry out (as my own ancestors first cried—for I am truly a Priest as well as a *chasid*—some two thousand years ago), "Can salvation come out of Galilee?" "Salvation always comes out of Galilee," I will answer out of the Chasidic side of my mouth: which is to say, it comes out of the quarter from which we Priests and Professors had least expected it, the world we find it easiest to despise: not some Galilee of the past that we have sanctified and made safe for ritual and research, but a Galilee of the future which we still revile and fear.

But the dialogue, after all, is in each of our own heads, as well as in the community at large, and it cannot stop here. For even knowing and confessing that salvation comes out of Galilee, perhaps only knowing and confessing that piece of the truth, we are not delivered of our priestly and professorial obligations, not permitted to cry like some mindless Gentile or wandering barbarian the matching slogan of contempt and terror "Can wisdom come out of Athens or Jerusalem!!" Wisdom *always* comes out of Athens and Jerusalem, which is to say, out of worlds clean, healthy, reasonable, and sane to the point of absurdity. Yet we dare not ignore the voice of wisdom when it insists, "The false prophet shall be put to death!" "The witch shall be put to death!" "The Messiah is yet to come!" "The Messiah is always yet to come!"

Only in the eternal tension of these two voices, Goyish and Jewish, prophetic and priestly, mad and sane, can the dearest of all possibilities be kept alive: the possibility (after the death and rebirth of the gods) of reinventing Man.

POSTSCRIPT (1996)

One of the plagues not mentioned in this essay, since it had not yet become visible, is, of course, AIDS. It is, however, foreseen, predicted, in a way that in retrospect seems to me almost uncanny. Certainly much of what I have written here about its minor forerunners casts light on this otherwise mysterious ailment. One of the centers, for instance, where it emerged and has continued to burgeon is San Francisco: the site of the "sixties" revolt against hygiene—and, indeed, against health itself. Most of the earliest victims were, to be sure, a new generation of white, male homosexuals. Nonetheless, the way in which they have not merely endured the disease, but flaunted, celebrated it—finally converting their resistance to efforts to control and cure it into a kind of cause—reminds me of the earlier efforts of the Counter Culture to make illness seem a protest against the bourgeois cult of health. So, too, it seems that this ultimate plague of the young can be understood as another physical manifestation of the culture shock resulting from a confrontation with an alien culture: this time that of pagan Africa, which in recent years has become a favorite refuge of "world travelers" in flight from the unendurably Christian America of their parents—thus teaching us once more that there are "no new Gods without new Diseases."

Pity and Fear

Images of the Disabled in Literature and the Popular Arts

❥❤

NOT TOO LONG AGO the adult "normals," chiefly male, who make such decisions for the United Nations decreed that each three hundred and sixty-five days we live be dedicated to one or another of the subgroups in society in relation to whom they feel most deeply conflicted—most guiltily aware of a discrepancy between their avowed attitudes and their covert prejudices. We have had in succession, therefore, the Year of the Woman, the Year of the Child, and finally the Year of the Disabled. The special difficulty of dealing with the last is revealed by the fact that it is not officially designated, like the former two, by one of its more common names, but by a euphemism apparently arrived at only after long debate. That euphemism, I must confess, is one which I (an aging patriarch myself, still able to pass as "normal") find it hard to remember, substituting for it before I am aware certain terms like "the handicapped" or "the afflicted"—now considered not merely old-fashioned but somehow offensive.

But names, I assure myself, matter less than the comic, horrific, or pathetic images which all of them, whatever the intention of their users, evoke at deep psychic levels, where up-to-date *logoi* are translated back into the archaic *mythoi* that underlie them. Such images have been fixed in song and story for a long time—as long, indeed, as humans have made literature. One of the chief Olympian gods, for instance, Haiphaistos, master craftsman and cuckolded husband of the goddess of Love and Beauty, was portrayed as lame and treated as a figure of fun whenever he deserted the smithy for the nuptial couch, thus reminding us that cripples were originally regarded as jokes. That tradition survived, in fact, up to the time of Shakespeare, who in *Troilus and Cressida* portrays the hunchback Thersites as a comic butt, laughed to scorn by the able-bodied warriors of the Trojan War. Moreover, Thersites remains a marginal character, scarcely more than a walk-on. And though in *Richard III* Shakespeare makes another hunchback, this time malefic rather than comic, central to the play, this is exceptional for the time.

Not until the late eighteenth century, with the rise of sentimentalism and the obsession with the excluded and marginal, which climaxed during the reign of Victoria, did the blind, the deaf, and the halt become major characters in books written by authors and intended for readers who, thinking of themselves as non-handicapped, are able to regard the handicapped as essentially alien, absolute others. In such a context, fellow human beings with drastically impaired perception, manipulation, and ambulation tend, of course, to be stereotyped, either negatively or positively but in any case rendered as something more or less than human. The disabled themselves, along with amateur do-gooders and those professionally committed to their well-being, are consequently tempted to dismiss such images as "myths" in the vulgar sense of the word, meaning damned lies.

However, to judge fairly the symbolic or archetypal roles that the crippled play in imaginative literature, we must understand what "myths" really are: namely, projections of certain unconscious impulses otherwise confessed only in our dreams, but which once raised to the level of full consciousness serve as grids of perception through which we screen so-called "reality." When these myths are embodied in literature, translated into words on the page or images on TV, they become a part of our daily experience, as "real" as any other. Precisely because of its mythic dimension, then, literature is radically different from other forms of verbal discourse, such as philosophy, history, journalism, or scientific reports. It is not intended to "tell the truth," i.e., to give reliable and otherwise verifiable information about the world outside of its texts.

Much less is literature obliged to persuade and reform us by showing us the error of our ways and moving us to right action. It does not even have to delight us, except to the degree necessary to prepare us for its proper function, which is to alter our ordinary modes of consciousness, to transport or enrapture us. It does this by releasing in us much that we customarily repress, thus making us more aware of, more at home with, certain dark responses to certain of our fellows—attitudes we tend consciously to despise, even to deny. In private dreams and nightmares, such responses and attitudes reveal themselves only obscurely, in encoded form, as it were; but in oneiric song and story, we perceive the repressed more clearly, since in reading or listening to literature we achieve—in the words of Henry David Thoreau—the privileged state of being "in dreams awake."

Mythic song and story provide us with a way of acting out, vicariously and thus harmlessly, attitudes that our avowed principles (whether based on politics, morality, religion, or psychology itself) tell us are socially undesirable, sinful, or pathological. I am not suggesting that literature serves to persuade us of the innocence of such impulses by making us believe that we ordinarily consider evil as, in some higher or merely different sense, good. It reveals to us rather that there is something in our psyches that stubbornly challenges whatever imperfect definitions of good and evil we may accept at any given point in time and space; and that this "something" is what is most truly and universally human about us. That realization, at any rate, makes us capable of ambivalence and irony (so prized by poets and so distrusted by prelates, politics, and ideologues); and eventually, therefore, helps prepare us to adopt new, also radically imperfect, codes of good and evil—to which, of course, we shall also fail to live up.

That endemic gap between that to which we aspire and that which we can achieve has been perceived by some artists as tragic and by some as comic. Whether it impels us to laughter or to tears, however, literature lets us accept our failure to realize our ideals without betraying us into bland self-deceit or blind self-esteem. Among other things, it tells us disquieting truths about our response to traditionally stigmatized segments of the population, including the disabled—revealing, beneath the benign tolerance that the more "enlightened" among us profess to feel, the primal terrors that beset them even as they do the least "enlightened." Reading novels, poems, and plays will not, let me be clear, exorcize those terrors; but by raising them to the level of full consciousness, it can deliver us from hypocrisy and make us aware of how little is altered by mere verbal changes: that superficial relabeling of which we tend to be so foolishly proud.

It seems to me only an easy way of appeasing the guilt we cannot really allay over our instinctive responses to men and women with drastic difficulties in ambulation to stop calling them "gimps" or "cripples" and refer to them instead as the "handicapped," the "disabled"—or, in that ultimately idiotic euphemism adopted after long heart-searching discussions at the last Democratic Presidential Nominating Convention, as the "challenged." I will not presume to speculate about how the lame themselves regard such euphemisms, though I suspect in many different ways, depending on how they have learned to live in the impaired bodies they inhabit.

I shall, therefore, speak here only for myself. Ever since I was a child, I have hated all euphemisms, beginning with those used by adults for the toilet functions (about which they talked to me constantly) as well as for sex, birth, and death (which they spoke of only behind my presumably oblivious back). Since attaining maturity, I have come to detest even more the polite terms for "oppressed minorities"—ethnic, generational, and sexual— imposed on the rest of us by political do-gooders. And I especially resent such linguistic censorship when applied to the epithets generally reserved for stigmatized groups to which I myself belong.

Certainly, as I approach the eighth decade of my life, my weight creeping inexorably beyond two hundred pounds and my Jewish heredity becoming ever more apparent, I discover that I would infinitely prefer to be described as a "fat old kike" than as "a portly senior citizen of the Hebrew persuasion." I do not, in short, need literature to remind me (though I rejoice to find it confirms my convictions) that nothing is gained by refusing to call a spade a spade in public, so long as in the darker recesses of our under-minds we continue to *feel* it a spade.

Furthermore, I suspect that what professionals in the field like to call "prejudices against the disabled" cannot be neutralized by the techniques of "behavior modification." Indeed such naive attempts at "scientific" brainwashing, it seems to me, tend, like semantic manipulation, to change what we say without touching what we dream. I am more inclined to believe that since they are renewed and confirmed by the mythic images of popular culture, such "prejudices" might possibly be altered by changing those images. There has been, in any event, a recent attempt of this kind, well-intentioned but too deliberate and heavy-handed really to work—and eventuating, therefore, in ineffectual stereotypes rather than truly effective archetypes.

I am thinking primarily of the wave of TV scripts and quickie films by which not so long ago we were inundated, in which a sympathetic protagonist is traumatically disabled, but emerges finally from an initial deep depression and learns to cope with life, love, work, and play. I find it difficult to identify with those protagonists, however, since they are portrayed not as ordinarily unattractive and inept human beings, but as super-beautiful super-jocks and jockesses. I suspect that my difficulty in this regard is scarcely unique. Surely, most viewers must, like me, inevitably feel themselves really handicapped in comparison with such splendid athletes. Such ersatz sagas of heroic "gimps," then, merely turn upside down rather than dissolve the sense of immitigable differ-ence which lies at the root of our troubled response to the disabled, by making them seem super- rather than subhuman. Worse, by their relentless emphasis on the positive, these stories exacerbate rather than release our negative feelings of hostility and guilt, leaving us finally more conflicted than ever.

The Jane Fonda film *Coming Home* represents a similarly unsatisfactory, though somewhat more pretentious, attempt to glorify the maimed. Part of the problem with this movie is that conscious politics preempts the role of unconscious fantasy, ideology supplanting mythology. Certainly this is true of everything in its plot, which sustains its thesis by presenting a paraplegic veteran of the war in Vietnam not just as fully human despite his disability, but as, thanks in part to it, a more-than-normally heroic protestor against "the System" and its apologists—all egregiously able-bodied, of course. Still, the film's simple-minded, sentimental politics, its implausible equation of militarism and patriotism with prejudice against the handicapped, surely does not explain the movie's wide appeal.

Though it may have pleased a minority segment (chiefly nostalgic survivors of the dissenting sixties), it could not possibly have touched most of the audience who made it a box-office success. What did move them, especially the women among them, whatever their conscious attitudes toward feminism, were certain genuinely mythic elements, long familiar in women's literature and quite unrelated to leftist politics. The first is the fantasy of making it with a cripple: a variant of the Beauty and Beast archetype, bred of the erotic horror-fascination (can they do it? how do they do it? how would it feel?) that drastically disabled males seem to stir in "normal" women. The second is a variant of the Cinderella archetype (classically formulated in Charlotte Brontë's *Jane Eyre* and present in American fiction from *Charlotte Temple* to *The Scarlet Letter*), in which the heroine gets the Prince only after he is maimed. Implicit in this mythic story, surely, is the belief that the best husband or lover is a maimed—which is to say a symbolically, though not really, castrated—one.

More successful, however—indeed, the most successful of all recent works dedicated ostensibly to redeeming the disabled from obloquy (while covertly delivering us "normals" from guilt)—has been none of the up-to-date attempts to elevate them to heroic stature, but a shamelessly old-fashioned celebration of the horror and pity of their plight. I am referring, of course, to Dr. Frederic Treves's autobiographical account of his dealings with John Merrick, the Elephant Man. Its popularity is attested to by the number of times it has been retold over the past several years: in a sociological study by Ashley Montague; in illustrated histories of physiological anomalies, like Frederick Drimmer's *Very Special People* and my own less euphemistically entitled *Freaks: Myths and Images of the Secret Self*; in the extraordinarily long-running play, which has been touring the country since its Broadway triumph; in an independently conceived movie, which attracted even larger audiences; and finally in a successful television version based on the play.

Certain elements present in Treves's account of a Victorian showfreak who became a medical curiosity and an occasion for conspicuous charity have been ignored or downplayed in these later recensions: most notably, perhaps, the curiously tender male bonding between doctor and patient that is its true erotic center. On the other hand, additions have been made in response to late twentieth-century taste and sensibility, whether academic or popular. Montague, for instance (apparently in contempt of the facts), used the case of Merrick to prove the importance of mothering to psychic health; the makers of the play sought to beef up its appeal with more properly heterosexual titillation and discreet frontal nudity; while the producers of the movie tried to ensure success at the box office by eking out the quiet pathos of the case with cops-and-robbers melodrama.

But despite the omissions and additions, the story remains essentially a Victorian fable about the triumph of enlightened sympathy and "scientific" health care (subsidized, of course, by the benevolent rich) over the irrational terror and loathing felt toward the handicapped, particularly by the lower orders. It constitutes, in fact, a sentimental bourgeois response in parabolic form, to the class war theories of Karl Marx, whom, we must remember, was also a Victorian.

Treves, however, did not actually publish his narrative about how he rescued Merrick, a grotesquely deformed victim of neurofibromatosis, from a life of neglect and exploitation until long after the reign of the Widow of Windsor was over. His book did not appear, in fact, until 1923, but the events he relates in it had occurred between 1884 and 1890, when Merrick died at age twenty-six, strangled by the weight of his own monstrously swollen head. Over that gap of some forty years, what had been for Dr. Treves lived life became dreamed legend; which is to say, actual events had been recast to conform to certain Victorian archetypes of the disabled that indeed possess us still.

Nor did it need the revival of the Elephant Man to reestablish them. Not only do they survive frozen into stereotypes on the screen, large and small, but most of the fiction dealing with the physically afflicted best known to the largest reading audience, including and especially children, even now dates from the Age of Victoria. It is, therefore, to it, rather than to what is chic at the moment, that we should turn if we wish to understand our own deepest reactions to disability. *Our* own, let me make clear (we TABS, as I am told those others call us, we "temporarily able-bodied"), not *theirs*; since what such stories tell us is not how the afflicted perceive themselves, much less what they really are like, only how we perceive them: those whom my grandmother—heir to a long mythological tradition—call the *Bestrafte*, the punished ones.

Reading Victorian literature, we find that, unlike the ancients who perceived them as comic, we respond to the maimed with what Aristotle argued were the feelings proper to tragedy, which is to say, pity and fear. These would appear to be contradictory, even mutually exclusive responses; but as we shall see, the one generates—or perhaps is somehow transformed into—the other. We begin, at any rate, with fear: terror, as my grandmother's ancient metaphor reveals, first of the cruel but just forces which make the disabled what they are; and then, in an odd act of displacement, of the disabled themselves. Sensing this, the disabled learn to play on it, exploiting it to extort alms, as the leprous beggars of Calcutta (and elsewhere) still do. What we experience as we flinch from their suppurating stumps—and if we do not realize this, literature reminds us—is not a rational fear of infection, but an irrational horror cued by their trauma and difference, the travesty of the divine image, which our religious tradition tells us is represented by the "normal" human body.

How easily such fear turns into hate: a hatred of ourselves for being unable to resist that shameful panic, then of those who stir it in us; and who, therefore, we tell ourselves—projecting what we cannot bear onto the "other"—must surely hate us for hating them. Finally, in the throes of paranoia and projection, we convince ourselves that the crippledness of the cripple is an outward and visible sign of an inward invisible state. Such nightmare delusions are classically embodied in the distorted Machiavellian king of Shakespeare's *Richard III*, a work that haunted the Victorian mind, providing a prototype for the innumerable maimed villains who follow. These include Quilp, the monstrous dwarf who stalks Little Nell through the pages of Charles Dickens's *The Old Curiosity Shop*; the one-legged, soul-seared Captain Ahab of Melville's *Moby Dick*, along with his blood brother, that smiling murderer with a wooden leg, Long John Silver of Robert Louis Stevenson's *Treasure Island*; the deformed, relentless cuckold Chillingworth in Nathaniel Hawthorne's *The Scarlet Letter*; and the ugliest cripple of them all, the protagonist of Victor Hugo's *The Hunchback of Notre Dame*.

Translated into twentieth-century horror movies, such twisted avatars of villainy (all played, it used to seem to me, by Lon Chaney) haunted my childhood. And they were succeeded by others, even more monstrous because more "modern": those maimed killers, who on stage, screen, and television, as well as in books, are portrayed as turning against us "normals" the prosthetic devices we have invented to alleviate their condition. Such technologically augmented monsters are already foreshadowed by the Captain Hook of James Barrie's *Peter Pan*; but they did not fully come into their own until they were reimagined by Ian Fleming and the scriptwriters of the James Bond films in those handless and toothless assailants of 007, whose artificial limbs and dentures are used as instruments of mutilation and murder.

The Bond villains tend to be portrayed as the tools of foreign agents, confusingly overlaying myths of the handicapped with the myth of the Cold War, or even of Alien Invaders from Outer Space. But like all their predecessors, they are adult males, older than those they threaten; which is to say, avatars of the sinister *senex*— bad fathers or wicked uncles, which every child recognizes under their transparent disguises of Pirates or Black Magicians or tyrannical Yankee Skippers. It is scarcely surprising that the handicapped be represented in oneiric literature by the figure of the Old Man; since in old age even the most "normal" among us is likely to become, like them inept, helpless—at the mercy of medical practitioners and our temporarily able-bodied relatives or friends. But even as we find ourselves in such a state at the end of our lives, so also do we at the beginning, when we are infants and small children. No wonder, then, that the child as well as the dotard, the *puer* as well as the *senex*, archetypally represents the cripple.

What is a little puzzling is that the latter stands for all in the disabled we fear and hate, the former for all we pity and cherish. It is tempting to explain the identification of the negative side of our ambivalence toward the maimed with the figure of the *senex* in terms of Oedipal resentment, everyman's hostility to his own father. But surely the association of old age with death, our sense that every ancient (and by the same token every cripple) is a living *memento mori*, must also have something to do with our response.

In any case, in mythic fiction the Bad Father typically dies before the end of the story—often at the hand of the child, that natural symbol of birth and renewal, whom he has begun by persecuting. So long as the archetypal child remains a girl, the erotic/thanatic relationship of the able-bodied and the disabled can be contained in the myth of Cupid and Psyche or Beauty and the Beast, in which the tabooed Old Man, the bestial father figure, is finally transformed into a princely and safely exogamous lover.

But somehow, beginning in Victorian times, that myth no longer satisfied the psychic needs of the audience; and we can see Dickens, sensitive to such exigencies, vainly struggling in *The Old Curiosity Shop* to turn the ancient story upside down by making the girl child (or at least some boyish ally) the murderer rather than the redeemer of the bestial cripple. Not, however, until the daughter is replaced by the son—presexual, androgynous, but mythically male—can the redemptive archetype be totally supplanted by the murderous one of David and Goliath or Jack the Giant Killer. And this is not finally achieved until James M. Barrie invents Peter Pan, that boy (always played, of course, by a girl) who will not grow up, never become himself a father, and is therefore able to kill the Evil Old Man without guilt.

Even as Barrie's archetypal tale allays guilt, it inhibits pity; since it permits us to feel sorry neither for the egregiously evil pirate he murders nor for Peter himself. An immortal *Wunderkind*, capable of flight, Peter stirs in us adults not the tender concern occasioned by the fragility and vulnerability of children but envy of the indefatigable energy of the very young and their unawareness that they will ever die. Certain other *puer* figures portrayed as cripples, though they are never killed to make a Happy Ending possible but rather miraculously healed, provide along their long-suffering way sufficient cause for tearful sympathy. Yet none of their stories is entirely unambiguous; since deep in the undermind of all of us there persists a desire to murder the disabled, even when they are infants, and even as we weep for them.

Indeed, long ago, obviously deformed children were ritually killed at birth. And though our religious beliefs no longer sanction infanticide, they still *are*, as we have been made aware by newspaper accounts of a child with Downs Syndrome whose parents permitted him to die. "Removal of life supports from non-viable terata" is the euphemistic phrase by which we refer these days to such drastic measures; arguing that not primordial terror has moved us, but an enlightened pity which prompts us to spare the hideously disabled (as well as those who love them) a lifetime of anguish. More typically, or so at any rate we would like to believe, we consign them to hospitals or to special "homes" away from home, most of them established in the Victorian era. But perhaps such sequestration represents only an alternative way of making the handicapped invisible, as good as dead. And even our attempts to "cure" or "repair" them, or with prosthetic devices enable them to mingle unnoticed in the world, may in part be the product of the same primordial fear of difference and monstrosity that once prompted ritual infanticide.

But surely there is a difference, we tell ourselves, since such latter-day strategies are motivated by pity rather than fear. Yet pity, the relevant literature seems to suggest, is only a disguised form of our aboriginal terror; and in any case it leads us to evade rather than confront the problem of our relationship to the disabled by tempting us into weepy voyeurism and self-congratulatory smugness. God knows how many hundreds of movies and TV shows have permitted us the sado-masochistic thrill of watching the suffering of the afflicted, sometimes even unto death, along with the sense that by doing so we are performing a virtuous act, proving that we *care* rather than hate or fear. That is most evident, perhaps, in *A Christmas Carol*, that prototype of all the tear-jerking melodramas about children, paraplegic war victims, maimed athletes, and loving wives afflicted with sudden blindness, which have become the staples of popular culture. And it helps to explain why Dickens's small, schmaltzy classic itself continues to haunt us, filling the shelves of children's bookshops and preempting the airwaves as each new yuletide approaches.

If there is an archetypal image of the handicapped stronger, more obsessive even than that of the sinister *senex* with a hump or a hook, it is that of the pitiful *puer* embodied in the crippled boy forever perched on Bob Cratchit's threadbare shoulder: "Alas for Tiny Tim, he bore a little crutch and had his limbs supported by an iron frame." Pale, microminiaturized, and presumably moribund, he threatens no one, only appeals for our sympathy and our help, calling on God to bless us every one whether we respond or not. It was his image that presided over the founding of charitable institutions (including the one that first asked me to meditate on this subject) to care for "crippled children." And his image has remained in the years since Victoria, when so much else has been desacralized, an icon as "sacred" in its way as that of the Christ Child at his Virgin Mother's breast; though also as vulgarly cheerful-tearful and as commercially viable as the Easter seal cripple-of-the-year, which descends directly from it.

What is most fascinating and revealing about Dickens's yuletide fable (aside from the fact that it managed to take Christ out of Christmas without offending the pious) is that in one of its two time sequences Tiny Tim dies, while in the other he survives. We are privileged, therefore, both to weep (with whatever covert relish) over his demise, his ceasing to exist, and to rejoice (with whatever secret regrets) over his ceasing to be a cripple. Dickens's tale, that is to say, provides us with two scenarios: in the first of which the *puer* is doomed by the refusal of the equivocal *senex* Scrooge, to render him the support owed by the able-bodied rich to the disabled "deserving poor"; and in the second of which, he learns to give what is due them "and infinitely more."

Oddly enough, however, though the author and the text ask us to believe that it is the latter Happy Ending that "really" happened, it is described only in a few grudging words assuring us that "Tiny Tim did NOT die..."; while the bleak alternative, despite the fact that it is presented as "only a dream," gets some two or three pages, as if to make clear that the purest, most disinterested pity tends to linger long over catastrophe, with which it is more than half in love. More consciously, of course, *A Christmas Carol* was written to persuade us that the plight of the disabled can always be alleviated by philanthropy, which is to say, money and love in the proper proportions.

Especially in Victorian times of high infant mortality and inefficient health care, that reassurance must have seemed more wish than fact. But that is the function of all mythic literature from fairy tales to soap operas, is it not? To allow us to "make believe" that we believe what we consciously know is not true—could, indeed, never be true, except in the realm of the "magic" or dreams, where wish is omnipotent. In that world alone, the neglected third sibling always triumphs, any ingenious beggar can become a king, all marriages continue "happily ever after," and the lame cast away their crutches and walk.

But the wish that is revealed in tales which evoke pity for the handicapped (including not just *A Christmas Carol* but such other childhood favorites climaxing in quasi-miraculous cures as *Heidi* and *The Secret Garden*) turns out to be disconcertingly similar to that which cues nightmare stories based on a fear of them; a wish that there were *no* handicapped, that they would all finally go away. In light of all this, it should be evident that traditional literary images of the afflicted contribute little or nothing toward creating attitudes which might make possible in actuality a society in which the disabled would be recognized as representing not some absolute, unendurable Other but one pole on a human spectrum, in which differences of perception and agility separate not merely one individual from another, but one stage from another in each individual's life, from the total dependency of infancy to the gradual crumbling of our powers in old age.

In such a utopian society, worked for as well as dreamed by committed professionals and amateurs of goodwill, all means of information retrieval and transport would be redesigned to accommodate such differences. Moreover, even the most debilitating handicaps would be perceived as constituting not a departure from, but another assertion of, the almost infinitely various human "norm." Even pain and early death would come to be faced head-on, tragically and joyously, rather than sniggered at in embarrassment, turned away from in terror, or denied in pity. But, of course, though we may be edging with painful slowness ever closer to such a utopia, we are not likely to achieve it fully until—once more as in fairy tales or dreams—wish is omnipotent. Until that time, we will have to exorcise our ambivalences toward the afflicted, whom to one degree or another we will continue to fail, by turning not to ersatz paeans to the heroism of the crippled, but to disturbing mythic literature; including *Richard III*, over which (let me confess) I still shudder, and *A Christmas Carol*, over which I have wept more than once—and will, I suspect, weep again.

Eros and Thanatos;
Or, The Mythic Ætiology of the Dirty Old Man

⇒✦⇐

MY SUBJECT IN THIS ESSAY is certain myths of old age—or rather, a myth of Old Age itself that is central to our culture. I propose to deal not with official mythology, the Scriptures of a sect—much less official mythography—scholarly interpretation of such Scriptures but with literature both popular and high: song, story, and drama, including movies and dirty jokes. In these forms, the myths and their meanings remain covert, implicit, and pass therefore into the deep imagination, influencing behavior and perception without ever posing the problem of belief. If we hope ever to understand how the old see themselves and are seen by others, at a level so far below the lintel of full consciousness that no effective rational challenge is possible, we must augment the insights of behavioral and medical science with the kind of illumination that only such myths can provide.

More particularly, I want to talk about myths of old men in love (I shall confine myself to males not just because I am one, but because our patriarchal culture has been concerned chiefly with them): "Dirty Old Men," we have come to call them, for reasons I shall try to make clear. The plight of mythic old men represents in extreme form the tension between *eros* and *thanatos*, carnal love and physical death, which determines the basic rhythms of our entire lives; and thus any meditation on the plight leads us to a heightened awareness of an absurdity underlying both comedy and tragedy: an absurdity that arises out of the conflict between the desire we cannot deny without denying the very wellspring of our existence ("We cannot cross the cause why we are born," says

Shakespeare), and the fragility of the flesh upon which the satisfaction of that desire depends. Such a perception of absurdity cannot be transcended without either the total renunciation of passion or a leap to faith—or both; if, indeed, it can be transcended at all.

The desire that represents one pole of this dilemma is typically represented in myths by the desirable Youth: the fatally beautiful Maiden or the irresistible Ephebe; and the weakness of the mortal body by the Old Man: the tremulous and decrepit graybeard, who though he stands on the verge of death seeks to forget it in the intoxication of a carnal embrace with such a Youth. In a culture like ours, which has traditionally endured repression and prized sublimation in the name of reason and self-control, the flight to the anodyne of sex has long been considered a second best for those of any age, and for the old totally inappropriate, especially when the desired partner is extremely young: since we do not merely ask that the old be treated with dignity, we (more dangerously) demand of them that they behave with dignity, impose decorum on them as a burden and a chore.

Such unions are felt by all of us nurtured on such myths (and who is not?) to be not only in principle taboo, but also likely in fact to prove ill-fated; since they represent a sin against ongoing life, which demands that the young marry the young—while the older generations withdraw from sexual competition and prepare for death, learn in short to be *properly old*. Even the most enlightened among us are likely to share this feeling, though we do not like to confess it, when we talk from the top of our ideological heads, rather than out of our viscera or the myth-ridden depths of the psyche.

To be sure, we can all cite cases where the ancient taboo has been broken with impunity, not only in the legendary or historical past, but right now; and not only by certain grizzled veterans, exempted by genius from what restricts ordinary men, like Picasso or Charlie Chaplin or Henry Miller, but by our own neighbors, ourselves. Yet when we fantasize or dream or relax into that unguarded receptivity into which mythic literature compels us, we hear again deep within the old saws, the old songs, "Crabbed age and youth cannot live together." *

I remember or half remember (and can pull down from my shelves to check out) phrases and scenes from favorite books of my own youth, some of which I have devotedly read and reread ever since, some that have long gathered dust. In Malory's *Morte d' Arthur* or in Tennyson's *Idylls of the King,* I encountered at age eight or nine the form of the myth that returns to me first: the story of Merlin, the aged Wizard of King Arthur's Court, who was charmed out of life though not into death, because he yielded to the erotic charms of Nimue or Nineve or Vivien—the name of his beloved scarcely matters, varying as it does from one version to another. What counts is that she be forever Young, even as he is eternally Old: "Half-suffocated," as Tennyson describes him, "in the heavy fell of many winter'd fleece on throat and chin"; and that, entwined in her snakelike arms, he betray to her his ultimate magic. Falling so inappropriately in love, he dooms himself to eternal imprisonment in a cave in Cornwall or the depths of a magical forest: symbols of the senile impotence from which not even death itself can deliver him.

From the melancholy of Arthurian Romance, I then turn, as I turned in my growing up, backward in historical time to Plautus and Terence, whose plays I learned as a college freshman to render into halting English. And I remember how we all laughed together in class, with a heartlessness appropriate to our age, even as the Roman audiences had laughed long before us with a heartlessness appropriate to theirs. And what joined us was a common

---

* There are to be sure literary works in which the marriage of Youth and Age is presented as a viable Happy Ending: in certain late novels of Dickens, for instance, and—at the very last moment—in Shakespeare's *Measure for Measure.* But such wishful projections have never assumed the status or ubiquity of true myths, i. e., widely shared communal dreams.

pleasure at the discomfiture of the *senex:* the Old Man (presented this time not as a revered Sage, but as a pompous householder, a foolish father, a buffoon) robbed by the wiles of his parasite and his son of some teenage Prostitute, for whom he had foolishly lusted. Indeed, the popular audience still laughs whenever that stock plot of the Defeated Dodderer is borrowed again by some contemporary hack, just as the Romans had borrowed it earlier from the Greek playwright Menander. What else, indeed, is *A Funny Thing Happened on the Way to the Forum:* a hit on Broadway and, in its movie version, in every small town in America?

That New Comic plot embodies a true myth of the eros of the aging: a myth of the Old Man defeated in his final hubris, as ancient as the culture of what we call the West—and as stubbornly long-lived. Even as I write, in Buffalo or Milwaukee or Newark, on tape or one some late, late-night TV rerun, Zero Mostel is still running through the streets of a Hollywood version of Rome to cheat the *senex* of his inappropriate bide, while the satisfied audience chuckles and guffaws. And if some among that audience, the ones already receiving Social Security checks, are somehow disturbed, they scarcely dare admit it even to themselves—lest in so doing they confess that they are the real occasions for the merriment.

They may, indeed, feel their own plight as more pathetic than comic, but most men in most times have considered comedy the proper mode for rendering the foredoomed defeat of Old Age in love. It was certainly Chaucer's preferred mode; though in his best-known treatment of the theme, "The Merchant's Tale," he presents it as the comedy of the old husband betrayed rather than that of the old father fooled: a version that still delights audiences, as certain scenes in Richard Lester's film *The Three Musketeers* attest. January and May, Chaucer allegorically names his ill-assorted pair: a reformed roué of more than sixty and the girl of less than twenty whom he has ill-advisedly chosen as the companion of his declining years. Like Lester, he conceals the pain of cuckoldry in farce—but he also tempers the farce with irony, thus doubly distancing the cuckold's distress. In "The Merchant's Tale," he maintains that ironic tone and the detachment it makes possible by telling his story through an obtuse misogynist who totally identifies with the aging husband.

Yet somehow, behind his unsympathetic back, Chaucer lets us surmise how it felt to the young bride to be possessed by so superannuated an erotic over-achiever—primed for the act by all the recommended aphrodisiacs and a desire to prove his unflagging powers. Though we are spared the details of their actual lovemaking, we learn how it seemed to her to wake and feel his half-shaven bristles on his cheek, and sitting up, to look down on his worn and withered frame. The real as well as the fictional narrator of the tale, however, was not a woman, young or old, but an aging man. And in the end, therefore, we must read the reactions attributed by Chaucer to May as projections of the unconfessed self-hatred and *Schadenfreude* experienced by an old man viewing himself in the mirror of a beloved young girl's eye.

I did not, indeed, realize at age sixteen what shame and guilt underlie Chaucer's presumably lighthearted tale—and how deep a yearning for self-punishment prompts the final scene of a cuckolding actually witnessed and improbably explained away. Yet just before that scene, as if to give us a clue, the King of Hell and his raped child bride, Persephone, appear. It is child rape, then, for which, at the level of fantasy and myth, the Old Man blames himself; though at the level of fact, he may only have seduced or persuaded or bought his bride, who moreover is a woman full-grown, however junior to himself. And in the popular mind, such fantasies become paranoic nightmares of the Dirty Old Man luring toddlers into back alleys with a lollipop.

Nor are such nightmares confined to barroom or *kaffee klatsch* gossip. Writers close to the mass mind, like Dickens and Dostoevsky in novels like *The Old Curiosity Shop* and *The Possessed,* have turned them into enduring literary images of terror.

And in the world of politics, Goebbels helped prepare the German people psychologically for the extermination of the Jews with a series of cartoons in which the dread figure of Father Abraham and the image of the aged violator of children are blended in a horrific unity. For so ultimate an offense, indeed, cuckoldry seems an insufficient punishment. It is death that is demanded, like the awful death of Quilp, the aging pursuer of Little Nell through the pages of *The Old Curiosity Shop;* or more commonly, since the archetype we are exploring seems to have a special affinity with farce and burlesque (even Quilp is finally a comic character), a death in bed, as lust proves too strong for the aging body it suits so ill.

"What a way to go!" male hearers of such tales are likely to comment—but behind their sniggering, there is a shudder, too. A shudder and a laugh. I must confess that like everyone else, I, too, even as I aged, kept laughing at such jokes; since that was one way of pretending that they are about someone else. Nor is it pretending only; for the other at whom we laugh is dead, and by laughing we know that we are not. Not yet.

Not that it is necessary, in order to remain inside the comic frame, for the girl involved to be completely blameless (obviously, in Chaucer she is not), merely that the *senex* be presented as the chief offender: contemptuous of the conventions by which our society has traditionally dignified both life and death. Comparatively, however, the girl must seem worthy of the Happy Ending which both the *fabliaux* and the New Comic versions of the myths provide: the Young in one another's arms—whether in casual intercourse in a flowering pear tree, as in Chaucer, or in the matrimonial bed till death do them part, as in Plautus and Terence. Only the Old Man stands alone—or rather *knows* he stands alone, as, indeed, he should have from the start. At that point the audience, satisfied by the ritual reaffirmation of the generational roles their own deeply buried lusts call into question, rise satisfied, to embrace each other in renewed innocence and laugh all the way home.

But it is quite otherwise in works embodying a myth in which the young girl bears the chief onus of blame—having functioned as a kind of second Eve in the new Fall of Man, irrevocable this time for having occurred in the evening rather than the morning of life. The legend of Merlin and Nimue, at which I have already glanced, is obviously a prototype of such tales, moving us to tears rather than laughter. And it is perhaps for this reason that it did not really come into its own in the English literary tradition until sentimentality had replaced irony and satire as prevailing modes. Malory had made very little of it in his fifteenth-century retelling of the Arthurian Romances; but in Victorian times, Tennyson moved Vivien and Merlin to the very center of a long poem on the same theme.

And that archetype has continued to obsess us, particularly as recast in certain popular movies made between World War I and World War II, in which the figure of Vivien blends with that of the "Vamp": that female creature of the Night, who, like her male predecessor, Dracula, sucks away the life of the victims of the opposite sex. Such films are replayed even now, in part because some of them can be considered, on formal grounds, "classics"; but in even greater part, because the mythic material they contain seems to us ever more relevant as more and more of us live longer and longer—sometimes long enough to outlive our original mates, more often long enough to exhaust the passion that originally brought us together. For such aging survivors, what we still like to call the new "sexual permissiveness" brings confusion rather than freedom; since by downgrading traditional ideals of continence and fidelity, it compels the elderly, when death draws nearer and physical beauty fades (in themselves and in their original mates), to keep performing the ever less convincing role of lovers with ever more incongruous partners.

The Blue Angel is for me the most memorable of such films; for in it the figure of the young Vamp (elsewhere degraded into the comic-strip stereotype of the Gold Digger mercilessly milking her

Sugar Daddy) is raised by the acting of Marlene Dietrich to the highest archetypal power. And it is similarly preserved beneath all the horseplay of the movie made from Vladimir Nabokov's *Lolita*—though the age of his heroine has been changed from thirteen to sixteen, thus losing one main significance of the novel. The astonishing success of Nabokov's book (his only best-seller, because alone among his books it evokes archetypal material available to the largest audience) is due, I am convinced, to the fact that in it he challenged, travestied, inverted the horror at the heart of the myth of Old Age in Love—the nightmare of child rape—by making the nymphet the seducer, and the old (or at least aging) male a double dupe for having believed to begin with that he was victimizer rather than victim.

At any rate, one function of both these films is to allay by displacement the guilt felt by elderly lovers; but, as it turns out, the guilt only and not the *shame*. Recalling *The Blue Angel*, I am aware how beneath its surfaces of misogyny, beneath even the fear of sexuality which that misogyny is intended to disguise, there persists a bittersweet celebration of the contempt felt, not by the sleek Sirens with unfallen breasts but by Old Men themselves, contemplating the ruin of their bodies, which our culture has taught them so extravagantly to prize and on which their self-definition as males depends.

The passage that most vividly expresses this self-hatred and the author's obscene joy in it is found in Thomas Mann's *Death in Venice*, a prescient little book published when he was not quite forty. "In the light of the sweet youthfulness which had done this to him," Mann writes of his aging protagonist, who at this point knows he is hopelessly, irrecoverably in love with a beautiful and indifferent young boy, "he detested his aging body. The sight of his gray hair, his sharp features plunged him into shame and hopelessness. It induced him to attempt rejuvenating his body and appearance. He often visited the hotel barber."

And then Mann renders one such scene with the barber, in

which Aschenbach is persuaded to disguise the fading of his flesh with cosmetics. "And like someone who cannot finish, cannot satisfy himself, he passed with quickening energy from one manipulation to another... In the glass he saw his brows arch more evenly and decisively. His eyes became longer; their brilliance was heightened by a light touching up the lids. A little lower, where the skin had been a leatherish brown, he saw a delicate crimson tint grow beneath a deft application of color. His lips, bloodless a little while past, became full, and as red as raspberries. The furrows in the cheeks and about the mouth, the wrinkles of the eyes, disappeared beneath lotions and creams. With a knocking heart he beheld a blossoming youth."

But, of course, Mann's victim-hero cannot grasp the elusive phantom of youth and beauty in a grotesque mask of youth and beauty that dissolves (as Mann never troubles to tell us), under the heat of the plague-ridden city through which he pursues the boy. Not until he learns what he—painted not like a lover but like a corpse—has really been pursuing, can Aschenbach attain his true desire. He last sees the madly desired youth on a sandbar, separated from where he sits in a beachchair by a strip of water, "a strongly isolated and unrelated figure with fluttering hair—placed out there in the sea, the wind, against the vague mists... And suddenly, as though at some recollection, some impulse, with one hand on his hip he turned the upper part of his body in a beautiful twist which began from the base—and he looked over his shoulder toward the shore. The watcher sat there, as he had sat once before when for the first time these twilight-gray eyes had turned at the doorway and met his own. His head, against the back of the chair, had slowly followed the movements of the boy walking yonder... it seemed to him as though, removing his hand from his hip, he were signaling to come out, were vaguely guiding toward egregious promise. And, as often before, he stood up to follow him. Some minutes passed before anyone hurried to the aid of the man who had collapsed into one corner of his chair..."

It is a conclusion tranquil and almost religious in tone, quite unprepared for, it long seemed to me, by the grotesqueness and horror of the immediately preceding scenes. Yet it is, at the deepest levels, satisfactory and even credible, like the improbably Happy Endings of Shakespeare's last plays: true if not to fact, at least to the wish that cues our dreams. Shakespeare, however, in spite of his own homoerotic sensibility, never granted to any of his homosexual lovers (think, for instance, of the two Antonios in *The Merchant of Venice* and *Twelfth Night*, closed out by the Happy Endings of everyone else, and abandoned on the empty stage without lines) the benison of a peaceful death. Indeed, the only equivalent I know to the last pages of *Death in Venice* appears in Ronald Firbank's now almost forgotten novel, *The Eccentricities of Cardinal Pirelli*, published in 1926. Dead at the age of thirty-nine but obsessed always by the eros of old age (the heroine of his first novel is 120), Firbank, like Mann, deals with the passion that drives a reverent and aged man vainly to pursue—in this case through the aisles of a baroque church—a teasing and heartless boy. We last see his obsessed Cardinal, dead at the foot of an altar, but beatific and presumably blessed, though stripped naked of all his regalia except for his mitre, and (we are led to surmise) unrepentantly erect to the end. "Now that the ache of life," Firbank tells us, "with its fevers, passions, doubts, its routines, vulgarity, and boredom, was over, his serene unclouded face was marvelous to behold. Very great distinction and sereneness was visible there, together with much nobility, and love, all magnified and commingled."

It is an ending which suggests that the most outrageous of loves—breaking those mythologically reinforced taboos which in our culture forbid the consummation he sought on the grounds of holy celibacy as well as the identity of sex—can itself be a sacrament: self-transcending, so long as it eventuates not in penetration and orgasm but in frustration and death. For a closed circle of upperclass English esthetes to which Firbank belonged in the years just after World War I, so paradoxical a conclusion may have worked; as it may work again for future generations, whose deepest fantasies and guilts have been radically altered by the Gay Movement and the revolt against the celibacy of the clergy. But how could I have responded to it: a good Jewish boy from Newark, New Jersey, headed—I was certain—for a life of heterosexuality and convinced that only the kind of Dirty Old Men who otherwise exposed themselves to little girls at play or sat with hats in their laps at pornographic movies could contemplate a union with a fellow male young enough to be their child. Indeed, for me, pederasty doubly compounded the heinousness of the act—as I suspect it still does, in their deep psyches, for many.

That this was not always the case, I knew well enough even then. And Mann reminds us of this when he permits Aschenbach to call his beloved Tadzio in the privacy of his own head "Phaedrus": a name that refers us back to the Platonic dialogue that opens with a discussion about whether it is better to be the lover—that is, old and wise like Socrates—or the beloved—that is, young and desirable like Phaedrus. And thinking of Plato, we are likely to remember the *Symposium* and the ancient Greek myth of Two Loves: one heterosexual, earthbound, and leading to marriage; the other homosexual, "heavenly," and eventuating in a relationship in which the older lover repays the younger for his carnal favors by instructing him in dialectic and a knowledge of the "true gods." Even for Plato, however, that second or "higher" kind of love still binds the lover to the material world until he learns to transcend his attachment to a particular individual and, indeed, to the flesh itself, by lusting only for the Ideal Form of Beauty, Beauty in the abstract.

In Judaeo-Christian culture, however, it is forbidden even to begin the ascent toward wisdom with a pederastic attachment; and in the secular culture which succeeds it, with any passion, heterosexual or homosexual, that joins the very old and very young. But *why*? Whence that basically irrational taboo? The answer surely must lie somewhere in the texts I have already evoked; but to unriddle them further I must go deeper still, back to more primal forms of song and story: back to the fairy tales that preceded them in history as well as the personal experience of us all.

Long before we read Malory or Tennyson or Shakespeare, much less Thomas Mann or Ronald Firbank, we were exposed to those old wives' tales in which some nubile girl is sealed in a tower, or set high on an unclimbable hill, or kept from marriage with someone her own age until an improbable task is accomplished or a riddle answered: kept, in short, in the power of the Old Man, *her* Old Man, who, indeed, proposes that task or asks that riddle. The incestuous base of such restraints is, though clearly implied, typically not made explicit in fairy tales, in which, despite their lack of secondary elaboration, a kind of primary censorship is at work. And in any case, what chiefly concerns the tellers of such tales is not the cause of the life-inhibiting taboo with which they begin but the means by which some Young Lover breaks through to the Happy Ending in which Boy gets Girl, which is to say, the Son wins the Daughter from the Father.

There are, of course, a few stories in which the Father-Daughter incest which cues the plot is stated overtly, most notably "Peau de l'âne" [The Ass's Skin], a favorite always of the French. Not only was it included in the first printed collection of such material, Perrault's seventeenth-century *Tales of My Mother Goose*; it was also turned into a movie for the Parisian Christmas trade in the early 1970s. And the *märchen* subplot in Shakespeare's *Pericles* reveals that the riddle asked by the wicked King Antiochus of the suitors for his daughter's hand deals precisely with their long-continued incest; for which, in due course, both father and daughter are burned to death by fire from Heaven. Indeed, Claude Lévi-Strauss argues (and I, for one, believe) that all fairy-tale riddles, whatever their manifest content, conceal the same guilty secret. "Between the puzzle solution and incest," he writes, "there exists a relationship, not external and of fact, but internal and of reason."

Moreover, when Sigmund Freud recast such mythic stuff as psycho-history in *Totem and Taboo*, he turned it into an account of the creation of the Nuclear Family by the imposition of an incest-taboo. In his latter-day fairy tale, the Ogre-Father-Chieftain is overcome by his sons, bent on depriving him of the right to breed new daughters out of his own daughters and daughters' daughters for as long as he survives. And to prevent such girls ever falling back into the hands of that "single powerful violent and suspicious Old Man" (the description comes to Freud from Darwin), those son-brothers ban him from possessing *any* young female in his power. But it is precisely such taboos which actual Old Men seem to threaten by reaching out to take—by dint of wealth or power or cunning accumulated in time—actual girls young enough to be their daughter. (Think, for instance, of those horrific scenes in Norman Mailer's *Deer Park*, in which the Movie Producer, the Old Man on his executive throne, forces some barely nubile starlet to kneel between his legs and satisfy his aging desires.

Nevertheless the lust of aging males—still fertile at an age when the women with whom they have grown old have ceased to ovulate—draws them, despite themselves, toward fertile girls they might have fathered; so that not merely the fantasy, most often punished in dream and story, but the fact, more often than not undetected and unpunished, of father-daughter incest persists still today in many parts of the world. It must be, then, its analogy with this abhorred yet irrepressible relationship that makes the passion of old men for young girls both suspect and alluring. But if this is the only, or primary, cause of the taboo we have been examining, why should their lust for young boys be felt as equally or more dangerous? (Not even Freud at his most flagrantly mythopoeic has suggested that father-son incest was once a part of human life.) James Joyce says on this subject a word from which it is hard to demur: "They are sundered by a bodily shame so steadfast that the criminal annals of the world, stained with all other incests and bestialities hardly record its breach. Sons with mothers, sires with daughters, lesbic sisters, loves that dare not speak their name, nephews with grandmothers, jailbirds with keyholes, queens with prize bulls..."

In light of this, it seems to me that the father-daughter incest-taboo represents not an ultimate ground of explanation for our fear of intergenerational sex but only another metaphor for the ultimate yearning of aging males to recapture simultaneously those beloved women of their youth whose flesh has withered with their own, and the mother they have never really known: the Virgin Mother, lost forever with the act of love to which they owe their own begetting, except as reborn in the Virgin Daughter, their sisters, or their own female children. The latter fantasy is captured with confusing religious overtones in Ingmar Bergman's *Wild Strawberries* and rendered more nakedly manifest in "The Ass's Skin," in which a Fairy Tale King promises to his Queen dying in childbirth to remain faithful to her memory until he meets a woman as beautiful as she—who turns out to be, of course, the very daughter whose birth has meant her death.

But also, and perhaps even more poignantly, the eros of old men yearns to repossess that ambiguous beauty they themselves once possessed—or come at least to believe in age that they did possess it in youth—attractive to male and female alike. If it is this lost androgyny they long to recapture, young males on the border between boyhood and manhood might well satisfy their desire better than any girl. But the kind of union between consenting adults of the same sex permitted these days by enlightened communities will not do. Only pederasty, a relationship between an older man and a boy, is an appropriate equivalent. The Judaeo-Christian tradition, however, has imposed upon that relationship a taboo even more fearsome than that which forbids incest. "He who has offended the least of my little ones, it were better for him that a millstone were about his neck and he were cast into the sea." No wonder, then, that in the hierarchy of mythological horrors, the rapist of little boys ranks even lower than the violator of small girls.

And yet a hunger so deeply implanted in us that it can be denied only by denying our full humanity demands to be rescued—not only from rigid and obsolescent morality but from the historical process in which subtle and ambiguous archetypes have turned into gross stereotypes, in which the aged man in love is vilified and caricatured. Such stereotypes serve to reinforce the indignities visited upon the aged by those whose perceptions of them are hopelessly warped by contradictory impulses with which they never quite come to terms. And worse, they reinforce the self-hatred of the aged themselves. Is there, then, no positive, life-enhancing way to get out of the trap—to transcend the conflict between the imperiousness of carnal desire and the fragility of the flesh?

In more traditional societies, ritual has presumably served such ends—that is, myth ceremonially performed rather than expressed in song or story. But my one brief encounter with a surviving rite of this kind has left me unconvinced that such a strategy could have made possible the degree of transcendence we nostalgically attribute to it. Or perhaps in present-day Nepal—where once I paid my rupee with her other worshippers and saw the seven-year-old Living Goddess plain—the ritual has become decadent as well as commercialized. In that time-trapped country, at any rate, an Avatar of the Goddess is still selected, when the occasion arises, from a list of girl-children born to certain qualified families. The candidates must be, first of all, very young, with many years still left between them and puberty, at whose onset their reign ceases; and they must also be able to look on unflinching as scores, even hundreds of sheep and goats are ritually slaughtered in an enclosed courtyard, until the blood of the sacrifice mounts up over their feet.

The girl finally chosen is ceremonially robed, her face painted in a mask-like simulacrum of something sexually alluring, though rather equivocal in gender. She is then confined for as long as her tenure lasts to the Sacred Chambers, where she can be looked at by many (for a fee, through a window and from below) but touched only by the aging Priests who practice with her, on her, certain Tantric sexual rites, about which much is whispered by the uninitiated but little precisely known. What is ceremonially reenacted in such rites seems to me to be the fantasy of child rape, the erotic myth of female innocence possessed by male experience. It is all, though, if not exactly chaste, at least genitally ambiguous and satisfactorily sterile since the Girl-Goddess is pre-nubile, and the Priests who possess her have been trained to withhold their semen in the act of love. Indeed, such retention of the seed is for the followers of the Tantric Way a supreme form of spiritual *askesis*, as well as a source of earthly delight: unendurable pleasure indefinitely prolonged—in this case, between the Old Man and the Child, the dying human and the immortal Goddess.

But the reigning Avatar is only ritually, mythologically divine, even before menarche; so that when recently the seven-year-old incumbent was visited by a journalist from India (a young woman, by the way), she gave the ritual game away. At first the Living Goddess spurned in dignified silence the candy with which her interviewer had hoped to bribe her into speech. At the very last moment, however, she grabbed it, crying to the interviewer's departing back, "Next time bring me a doll"—which is to say, a symbolic baby to mother and nurse. But even after she has been declared empty of the Divine Presence and released to the secular world, the ex-Avatar—despite the fact that it was the onset of fertility that ungodded her—is unlikely ever to have a real baby. Whatever the Old Priests may declare, she remains for ordinary males forever taboo, precisely for having performed over and over with those Priests the nightmare of child violation. Indeed, the two of the Avatars who preceded the reigning Goddess are, at the present moment, working the streets of Kathmandu as prostitutes, which seems to me somehow fair enough. After all, aren't whores, no matter how young and attractive, available to all men with their price in hand, no matter how old and hideous? And do they not, therefore, represent in fallen form a ritual more ancient even than that of Nepal; in which on the steps of the Temple of the Great Goddess her acolytes honored with their bodies all males still potent and willing, no matter how close they stood to death.

And that ritual persists among us still, though it has grown ever more degraded as the whorehouse has replaced the Temple and the act once considered sacred has become a dirty joke. Reflecting on the theme, I find myself recalling in an odd but somehow appropriate conjunction scenes from my earliest adolescence, when—in the same candy store where "eight-pagers" (erotic parodies of current comic strips) were peddled under the counter, and the corner cop was nightly implored to lay his magnificent *shlang* on the table to be wondered at by all—two old lechers called, like a pair of burlesque comedians, Klein and Schlein (how incredibly ancient their sixty-five or seventy years seemed to me at fourteen or fifteen) would talk, making the only poetry in their power, about some young girl they had bought the night before, moist and open as their wives no longer were: some fabulous *shikse* "with a *tuchas* as white as gold." And how could I know—any more than they— that it was an Avatar of the Goddess whom they sought in parody. I only despised them then as Dirty Old Men, believing that so close to their own deaths the heyday of their blood should have been long since tamed.

Ignorant kid, I had not yet learned (and what would I have done with the information in any case?) that the Triple Goddess in her third and final form is called not just Persephone but *Kore*, meaning the Daughter; and that in this form she presides over the laying out of the dead—stands, in fact, for Death itself: Death as Love, Love as Death, the Daughter as Death. I do not, however, consider such a theological interpretation of the myth a satisfactory ending to my search, only another metaphorical simplification of the mystery: a way of achieving peace not by a true resolution of warring *eros* and *thanatos* but by the elimination of one of its poles. "If the eye offend, pluck it out." It is to a poet, therefore, rather than a prophet or a priest that I propose to turn in conclusion—to Shakespeare, who all his life long wrestled with the problem of "crabbed age" in love with youth; and who in *The Tempest* came as close as any man can to transcending the dilemma that relationship figures forth.

From the beginning of his career, Shakespeare confronted the dilemma in its two primary mythic forms, as pederasty and incest: the love of an older man for an unattainable boy, and the strange unwillingness of fathers to release their nubile daughters to marriage and motherhood. About the former, the society he lived in was equivocal; for though the Church condemned it and the State theoretically exacted the death penalty for practicing it, overt homosexuality was the preferred erotic mode of much of the aristocracy and of James I himself; while the neo-platonic Academies of the time called on the *Symposium* to justify their contempt for women and their preference for each other. Besides, the theater of Shakespeare's day was a constant provocation—with boy actors playing sometimes boys and sometimes girls, but especially girls pretending to be on stage the boys they really were off it: boy-girls, girl-boys—fit symbols for youthful beauty and the unlimited possibilities of polymorphous perverse pleasure.

Yet in the most confessional of all his works, *The Sonnets*, Shakespeare makes it clear that even the notion of a "pure" or Uranian Love, which is to say, homosexual love without final physical consummation, is a delusion and a trap: a way to mutual betrayal and self-deceit; since what it really embodies is a desire to end all begetting, which is to say, total death. And in the mouth of Antonio—Shakespeare's surrogate in *The Merchant of Venice*, who in his heart wants to abort the Happy Ending of the play by keeping Bassanio for himself—Shakespeare passes sentence on all in his own heart which is similarly inclined. "I am a tainted wether of the flock," Antonio says, "meetest for death." But even Antonio's desire to die for his beloved youth Shakespeare seems to find a last sentimental self-indulgence. And he grants him, therefore, no such consummation—only abandonment and a continuing life alone, when at the close Bassanio gets Portia, or rather, she him.

With the meaning of father-daughter incest, however—especially in its typically attenuated form of "All right, marry then, if you have to, but not *him*," or "Say at least that you love your papa more"—he apparently had more difficulty in coming to terms. Whatever sympathy he expresses for those of his young heroines who flee their fathers for their lover's sake, he seems to have found it hard to let them escape scot-free. Some, to be sure, he permits conventional Happy Endings, when the New Comic form of his inherited material offers him no alternative. But he condemns as many more to death, when the plot can be wrenched to allow it: not only in tragedies like *Othello* ("She has deceived her father and may thee," Iago says, preparing for the bloody dénouement), *Hamlet,* and *King Lear* (in which Shakespeare actually changed the ending of his source in order to give Cordelia her due come-uppance) but even in that odd failed comedy, *Romeo and Juliet.*

Only late in his life, when writing *Pericles*, did Shakespeare become fully aware that what had seemed to him earlier, in the continual father-daughter crises of his plays, chiefly the fault of the strong-willed daughter is primarily, or even solely, the responsibility of the father. Like those fictional fathers, Shakespeare was for a long time unable to realize the implications of his reluctance to relinquish his child to someone of her own generation, whom she might love more dearly and who would in any case outlive him. But contemplating the mythic materials in the old legend of Apollonius of Tyre, on which he drew for *Pericles*, he seems to have learned that the desire to keep the daughter implies also the desire to beget on her new daughters and on them new daughters still; which in turn implies an unwillingness to accept one's own death, a delusive dream of immortality in the flesh. The mythic meaning of father-daughter incest, then, seems to be in one sense the opposite of that of pederasty. But in another, deeper sense, they are complementary, two sides of a single coin; since both the dream of embracing death in the form of a beardless boy and of forestalling it indefinitely in the arms of an ever-renewed bride represent a refusal to grow old, to accept man's fate. "We must endure our going hence even as our coming hither," Shakespeare had already written at this point, but that wisdom both the pederast and the incestuous father deny.

Not so Prospero, of course, who at the beginning of *The Tempest* has been granted by a series of events beyond his control the dream of all concupiscent fathers: finding himself as old age approaches the sole human male on a desert island with his nubile daughter. To be sure, there is also Ariel, a spirit of air and fire, which is to say, a duplicate *anima* figure to Miranda, and one almost equally dear to him. Indeed, Prospero bestows more endearments on him than on her; for Ariel is a "he," a boy-actor, in fact, though he plays only female parts in the little plays that Prospero mounts within the larger play and is usually portrayed by a woman on the modern stage. He symbolizes, in short, the fulfillment of the pederast's fantasy in which the beloved boy is no heartless flirt but a slave subservient to his master's every wish.

And finally, there is that grosser spirit, Caliban: the would-be rapist of Miranda, whom Prospero from time to time forgets, wants to forget, since he stands for dark incestuous wishes in himself which up to the last possible moment he resists admitting. It is, however, the unexpected reappearance of that phallic monster that disrupts his Wedding Masque: the pageant which so improbably envisages a union of male and female, fertile and long lasting but without passion. And the unforeseen interruption reminds him therefore not only of the absurdity of his Eutopian vision of marriage but also (for reasons which should be clear at this point) of the fact that he has grown old and feeble and must therefore complete his task without delay. "Bear with my weakness," he says to his prospective son-in-law, just after Caliban breaks in on them both, "My old brain is troubled. Be not disturbed with my infirmity."

And what remains to do in the little time left him is precisely to destroy the self-serving double dream of earthly bliss with which the play begins: to disenchant his enemies and give away to one of them (the chosen lover of the daughter belongs always, mythologically speaking, to the enemy camp) his beloved Miranda; then to free his "chuck," Ariel; and by adjuring the potent magic which can make reality conform to wish, or seem to ("I'll break my staff... And deeper than did ever plummet sound / I'll drown my book..."), insure that his return to the real world of Naples and Milan can never be revoked or reversed. In that world, he foresees himself not just presiding at the going-away of his daughter, so long feared but finally, with only token resistance, allowed; but beyond that, devoting his last days to meditating on his impending and now accepted end: "And hence return me to my Milan, when / Every third thought shall be my grave."

Only Caliban cannot—even at the moment of reconciliation and acceptance—be given away to another or remanded to the elements from which he came; for unlike Miranda and Ariel, that rebellious creature dreaming the daughter's rape is bound to Prospero till death do them part. "This thing of darkness I / Acknowledge mine..." Prospero is driven at last to admit, thus confessing that the uncontrollable sexuality which has threatened both his own dignity and the innocence of his daughter is something neither monstrous nor alien but human and his own. And what, then, is left to add, as he stands alone with this hard-won wisdom on a stage deserted by all the other characters; what, except the even more difficult truth, which that first confession has somehow made easier to confront:

> ...Now I want
> Spirits to enforce, art to enchant,
> And my ending is despair
> Unless I be relieved by prayer...

More Images of Eros and Old Age:
The Damnation of Faust and the Fountain of Youth

⤜❦⤛

SEVEN YEARS AGO (as I was entering the sixth, the mythological last decade of life) I found myself speculating on what it meant to have become, not just in the eyes of others but in my own deepest imagination the "Dirty Old Man," traditionally portrayed in song and story as vainly pursuing some barely nubile and, therefore, *taboo* youth. Even in our presumably "liberated" time, I began to suspect, when we are urged to keep up an unflagging sexual performance to the very verge of the grave, there still persists in us a feeling that such a performance is not merely foredoomed but unseemly as well.

It was not, however, until I reached my sixty-fifth year that I realized just how deeply conflicted we are on that score. And how could I not, considering that since becoming officially one of the "Golden Aged" I have been reminded of that fact by unsolicited mail from companies who in an attempt to make a fast buck evoke images of *eros* and *thanatos* from both sides of that double bind. Some of their letters—offering special deals on life insurance without physical examination or bargain cemetery plots and caskets—exploit the prescience of impending death implicit in the Myth of the Dirty Old Man: the awareness of our mortality that simultaneously exacerbates and cools the desire of the old to couple with those so young they do not yet know they will ever die. Moreover, like that archetypal tale, they urge us "to go down dignified," to "Provide! Provide!" against the loveless eternity that lies beyond the brief span of loving and begetting which is our life in time. "Find out all the advantages of mausoleum crypt ownership

NOW…" one such leaflet reads. "If you plan ahead the decision can be made without the pressure of emotion."

How debased and trivial and essentially false are assurances that we can thus confront the threat of death without troubling emotion—shorn, as they are, of the traditional promises of immortality or the hope of Heaven. Only the guarantee of "perpetual care" for the gravesite to which our ashes will be consigned is provided. Yet somehow these secular travesties of consolation have for me the same kind of baleful fascination as the obituaries in the daily newspapers and the alumni magazines of schools I have attended, which I consult to see what old friends have predeceased me and how many total strangers of my own age or younger have already died. Contrary to what they seem to promise, however, such ads instead aggravate rather than allay the primal *timor mortis* we are heir to. But, perhaps precisely because of their banality, their final effect is to exorcize the bad dreams stirred in me by the myth of *Eros* as *Thanatos*—in which I am unsure whether the lovely ephebe I pursue in rapid eye motion sleep is the image of my irrecoverable youth or that of my inevitable demise.

In any case, I arise the morning after oddly refreshed, delivered from my oldest incubus. "Let the dead bury their dead," I declare to whomever will listen; and "We must endure our going hence even as our coming hither." Then I go to my mailbox prepared to heave the latest installment of commercial *memento mori* into the wastebasket unread. But looking down, I see that the new day's batch of mail "for elderly eyes only" is disconcertingly different from what I had been expecting. The letterheads this time read not "For Lawn Cemetery and Mausoleum" but "S/40," meaning, I discover, sex after the age of forty. And the large print on the cover of the enclosed brochure raises the ante even higher, assuring me that "'The One a Night' pill ensures maximum erotic satisfaction for men in their 40s…50s…60s…70s…80s. And even older." "Age is no longer an excuse for 'sexual senility,'" it goes on, the tone now halfway between reassurance and mild rebuke. "You can have the power to love no matter how old you may be." And lest any still remain doubtful, there are signed testimonials from satisfied users of Corazine-DL or NSP-270, written in language simple and gross enough for the least literate. "I am 69 years old. Since I started your pills…I want sex every day…" "I can get a hard and long lasting erection—so long that my wife was going to hide my pills…but I don't let her know where I keep them." "I am 76. After the first 30 capsules, my penis became firm. I am proud of it and when I urinate I think I am holding someone else's."

It is tempting to dismiss such crass appeals as irrelevant to anyone but the pathologically insecure; and yet I must confess that from the start I sensed behind them the presence of a myth of eros and old age, especially appealing to our time and place perhaps, but surely ancient in its origins. Superficially, they seem based on a naive faith—very twentieth-century, very American—that science can cure all the ills of our flesh; plus an equally unquestioned modern belief that one of those ills—the supreme indignity, in fact, that befalls us as youth departs—is the loss of potency. Such advertisements, though they make a show of being addressed to women as well as men, clearly speak primarily to males, who, in a time that considers sexual inadequacy more unseemly than indecorous lust, are in a particularly difficult spot. Wearing as they do the physical sign of erotic readiness in full sight, they can deceive neither themselves nor their partners when "sexual senility" overtakes them.

But in *any* time since we separated ourselves from other mammals by divorcing sex from periodic estrus, the fear of being eventually unable to get it up, of failing to cut the mustard, must surely have haunted the males of our species, leading them to seek—in eternally deluded hope—some nostrum or charm or spell that might guarantee perpetual potency. True enough, in the heyday of Orthodox Christianity, when the devout were taught to pray for deliverance from desire rather than to regard its inevitable waning as a disaster, that primordial fear and the delusive hope it begot were seldom publicly confessed. It is hard to believe, however, that they did not live on, subliminally at least: finding expression, like other repressed human responses, in the encrypted form of myth.

Indeed, though I somehow failed to notice it in my earlier essay on the topic, "Eros and Thanatos" (for reasons which will become clear before I am through), there *is* in our tradition a myth which reveals the dialectical interplay of ambivalences created by the tension between our natural dread of sexual failure and the teachings of the Church. Beginning with a nightmare evocation of impotency in old age, that archetypal story turns in its second stage into a wish-dream of restoring youth and genital vigor with a magic potion; then lapses into a night-terror again as the miraculous recovery turns out to have been a hoax or a diabolical trap. In its classic form, this story has been reembodied over and over by dramatists and poets and musicians, including Marlowe, Goethe, Valéry, Gounod, and Berlioz. Nor has it ceased to haunt us in post-Gutenberg times, being reimagined in such movies as Brian De Palma's *Phantom of the Paradise.*

Like everyone else in the dying twentieth century, therefore, I have long been haunted by that archetypal tale. In fact, I once acted the part of its protagonist in a production of Valéry's *Mon Faust,* which is in truth quite explicitly erotic. For a long time, though, I thought of it not as a fable of *eros* and old age but solely as a myth of the *hubris* and consequent damnation of the scientist: the prototype of certain pop classics of the nineteenth century like *Frankenstein* or *Dr. Jekyll and Mr. Hyde,* as well as the pulp fiction and comic books of the twentieth century, in which the modern Prometheus becomes the caricature of the "Mad Scientist" plotting the destruction of the world but achieving only his own.

Very early on, however, the myth of Faust—the "studious artisan," who is archetypally old—was conflated with that of Don Juan, the indefatigable sexual athlete who is archetypally young. That process had already begun with Marlowe, whose Dr. Faustus, though not really aged, is nonetheless seeking in his forbidden studies a sexual New Life. Despite all his grandiloquent talk about wanting to "make the moon drop from her sphere" and "the ocean to overwhelm the world," what he actually asks for once he has sealed his infernal bond, is "a wife, the fairest maid in Germany." Moreover, his final request of Mephistopheles is to "have unto my paramour / That heavenly Helen," the erotic ideal of pre-Christian paganism. Domestic bliss is apparently not in the power of Marlowe's Devil to bestow; what he can grant the amorous doctor—and even this perhaps only in illusion—is a kiss from Helen which sucks away his soul. Though this seems to me an anticlimax to his vaulting ambition, verging indeed on absurdity, no reader, I think, has ever managed to laugh at it; since most of us have continued to dream to our own day the Faustian wet dream, believing on some level, whatever our conscious morality, that sexual consummation is more devoutly to be wished than the power to reorder the Cosmos or confuse the Elements.

That dream was, at any rate, still being dreamed by Goethe, when at the end of the eighteenth century (at the very moment America and Romanticism were being invented) he wrote the first version of a poetic drama he spent the rest of his life emending and revising. On a conscious level, he sought at first only to turn the story of Faust into a bittersweet tale of seduction, sentimental and domestic enough to please the bourgeois taste of his own times. But before he was through, he had, without quite knowing it, turned it into a myth of Endless Love, in a form that would still remain viable when damnation had become a metaphor, sex was no longer regarded as sinful, and earthly science had begun to inspire the faith formerly reserved for God.

Goethe first accomplished this transformation of the archetype by making his Faust unequivocally old—and then grafting onto his legend that of the Elixir of Life or the Fountain of Youth, which had long flourished independently, particularly in the lore of the Alchemists. Goethe's Faust, that is to say, is rejuvenated only after he has quaffed at a Witches' Sabbat a "filthy brew" that takes twenty years off of his life. There has been no doubt from the start about why he seeks thus to reverse the process of aging; since Mephisto has assured him that if he takes his medicine he will learn once more "with intensest pleasure / How Cupid stirs within and bounds about..." And this time the Spirit which Denies keeps his promise; providing the rejuvenated Doctor with a real, live, flesh-and-blood girl: a village Fraulein, "decorous...virtuous...a little pert as well," and, best of all, eminently seducible.

Though the actual seduction of an all-too-human Gretchen seems at first an even more comic anticlimax to the Faustian quest than the illusory possession of a ghostly Helen, it, too, ends in terror. First the child she bears to Faust dies at her hand, then Gretchen herself perishes—leaving him still young but lonelier than ever and burdened with guilt. It would appear that the horror with which Christianity had taught the pagan world to regard unbridled passion ("the wages of sin is death") persisted still in the unconscious of Renaissance atheists like Marlowe and apostles of the Age of Reason like Goethe. Not even in America, which had declared its independence from the traditional belief systems of Europe, were writers delivered from the Faustian nightmare of damnation. Not for quite a long time anyway.

And how could they have been, since two hundred years before the appearance of the Deists who framed the Declaration, New England had been settled by a generation of true Believers, who read side by side with the Bible, *Pilgrim's Progress* and *Paradise Lost*, chapbooks containing the legend of Faust. Small wonder then that as late as the mid-nineteenth century, the image of the Satanic Pact is still to be found at the center of the novels we have come to consider the masterworks of the period. The secret motto of *Moby Dick*, Melville confessed, was "I baptize you not in the Name of the Father, the Son and the Holy Ghost, but in the Name of the Devil": and Hawthorne spoke of his *Scarlet Letter* as a "hell-fired book." Nor did these descendants of the Puritans ever suggest—like Goethe in the final version of his *Faust*—that their

Fausts would be somehow ultimately saved. Captain Ahab goes down to destruction with blasphemy on his lips; and Chillingworth becomes the Dark Spirit he serves, "a serpent manifest."

To be sure, a countermyth of rejuvenation without guilt, a dream of finding an innocent Fountain of Youth without diabolical aid, has also possessed the American imagination from the start. Even before the WASP founders of New England had sought to persuade the Indians of the icy North that sex without marriage was a sin, explorers from Southern Europe had sought to discover from the aboriginal inhabitants of Florida the exact location of those miraculous waters. It was, indeed, the hope of finding that Fount which persuaded them in the first place to dare the dangers of the Atlantic crossing. Moreover, though their mythic quest failed literally, it succeeded symbolically: creating an enduring image in the deep psyche of the world of Americans as New Adams and Eves, eternally young in the Garden of the New World. That we ourselves have introjected that image is attested by the fact that on the very beaches where Ponce de Leon once sought the fabled waters we can find at this moment withered refugees from winter and their own senility acting out in unsuspected caricature the myth of eternal youth. Meanwhile, all up and down America, other aging Americans pursue rejuvenation by sipping Geritol, popping Vitamin E, dieting, jogging, or submitting their sagging flesh to the cosmetic surgeon's knife.

The whole foredoomed effort represents, in one sense, the quest for a kind of ersatz immortality in the flesh, with which we have sought to satisfy ourselves since the death of God and the loss of the hope of Heaven. But specifically for the aging, it represents also and chiefly the dream of turning back the clock permanently; which is to say, not only of becoming young and potent once more but of staying that way. Moreover, we have now persuaded ourselves that such a reversal of entropy does not require, as in the Faustian legend, striking a bargain with Evil and eventually paying the price; since presumably lily-white Science can now provide without the risk of damnation (in which we no longer believe) what Black Magic so delusively and dangerously promised. Science or quasi-science or, at the very least, pseudo-science—including the nostrums of the pillpushers, the behavior-modification techniques of sexologists like Masters and Johnson, the psycho-therapy of Freud and Jung and Wilhelm Reich—has, in short, become for us the true Fountain of Youth, the new Alchemy.

Indeed, in the popular mind, Dr. Freud has long since achieved a mythological status almost equivalent to that of Dr. Faustus: feared by some as one more subverter of the moral order in league with the Powers of Darkness but seeming to many more a secular savior, capable of "scientifically" delivering us all from repression and impotence. Freud, however, though he did teach that "full genitality," erotic maturity, was a blessing rather than a primal curse, was essentially a believer in sublimation and restraint, a champion of monogamy and the nuclear family. And despite this, advocates of sex without responsibility or guilt evoked his holy name in the decades just before and after World War I. Finally, a new generation of Sexual Revolutionaries appeared after World War II, to whom "sublimation" and "maturity" were dirty words—when in short the Sexual Revolution and the Youth Revolution were fused into one—they turned away from the Founding Father of psychoanalysis to his most heretical ex-disciple, Wilhelm Reich.

Half shaman, half scientist—and in the end, quite mad—that apostate from Freudian orthodoxy became a major influence on certain Jewish-American novelists of the fifties: most notably Isaac Rosenfeld, Saul Bellow, Paul Goodman, and Norman Mailer, whom he persuaded that sexual repression is the cause of all the ills that beset us—not only neurosis and impotence but cancer and capitalism and war. Reich preached, moreover, and such writers believed, that the way to salvation, both personal and social, was to seek with the aid of Orgone Therapy (and to celebrate in fiction) the Perfect Orgasm. Inevitably, the Reichian redefinition

of love "as the search not for a mate, but…an orgasm more apocalyptic than the one which preceded it" led to a detachment of *eros*
from the myths with which it had been traditionally associated,
like that of Romeo and Juliet or Tristan and Isolde or even
Cinderella. Instead, it was associated on the one hand with the
Quest for the mythical Holy Grail and on the other with the legend of the Fountain of Youth.

In Mailer's essay "The White Negro, Superficial Reflections on
the Hipster" (the closest thing to a manifesto produced by the
generation of Reichian apologists), the latter identification is
spelled out in full. "It is not granted to the hipster to grow old
gracefully—he has been captured too early by the oldest dream of
power, the gold fountain of Ponce de Léon, the fountain of youth
where the gold is in the orgasm." But, of course, both Grail and
Fountain are ultimately unattainable; which is to say, the dream
of youth and potency eternally restored never dies because it is
never fulfilled. This Mailer himself goes on to confess ("the apocalyptic orgasm…remains as remote as the Holy Grail"); but he is
wrong about the cause—suggesting that such failure is due to
remaining knots of neurotic violence in the "hipster," which
inhibit full genital release. No, if the myth itself begins with hope
and ends in frustration, this must be because we have all of us
always, on some level or other, *wished* it so; since the wish is father
to the dream.

Only in the mythic imagination of the self-hating WASP is even
the "Negro" immune to the desire to be delivered from the endless
round of tumescence and detumescence by growing old. And
Mailer, far from being a "Negro," is a "Jew"; which is to say, his
archetypal opposite not just in the deep psyche of the Gentile
world but in that of all Jews exiled in that world. Who of us educated in the United States, Gentile or Jew, is not possessed by the
archetypal image of Shylock—the castrating Old Man, the
Patriarchal Enemy of Young Love, threatening the innocent eroti-
cism of pre-Christian Europe with the knife he is eternally

whetting on his boot, the Law in whose name he claims to speak: "Thou shalt not commit...," "Thou shalt not covet..."

Nor does it help much that Mailer has ostensibly rejected his Judaic heritage, embodying his erotic fantasies in prepotent goyish protagonists and declaring himself heir apparent to antisemitic Ernest Hemingway. The literary tradition out of which Hemingway comes is, whatever Mailer may believe, a Puritan one, which from the start sought to subvert the myth of the Fountain of Youth. The earliest story I know, for instance, in which a major American author deals with that myth is Hawthorne's "Dr. Heidegger's Experiment," which opens with the good doctor offering to four aged friends, three men and a woman, a potion he claims was drawn from the fabulous Fount. Typically, Hawthorne leaves some doubt about whether this claim is literally true; but it scarcely matters, since the waters *work*, psychologically at least. In a very little while the author tells us, "they were young: their burning passions proved them so"; which is to say, lust and jealousy soon has the males, inflamed by the restored "witching beauty" of the withered hag with whom they had entered, at each other's throats. But even as they struggle, what is left of the potion spills and they find themselves old again. "The Water of Youth possessed merely a virtue more transient than wine," Hawthorne comments editorially; and Dr. Heidegger concurs, declaring, "I bemoan it not, for if the fountain gushed at my very doorstep, I would not stoop to bathe my lips in it. Such is the lesson you have taught me."

Long before Hawthorne ever made it into print, however, American writers had already learned that lesson, which few of them have ever forgotten. Indeed, the first mythological character created by an American author to succeed in capturing the imagination of the world was Washington Irving's Rip Van Winkle; and he—fleeing rather than seeking a wife—adds rather than sheds the Faustian twenty years, leaving him safe on the further side of passion. The only other figure in our literature of equal archetypal resonance is Huckleberry Finn, whom Mark Twain imagined—

dreaming himself back twice twenty years to when he himself was a boy—fixed forever in "innocent" boyhood; or in other words, safe on the *hither* side of sexual maturity. Small wonder then that at the heart of many native works we especially cherish, similar anti-Faustian protagonists appear: old before their time, or younger than they have any right to be, but in any case, impotent. Think, for instance, of Cooper's eternally virginal backwoodsman, Natty Bumppo, evading marriage like Civilization itself; of Poe's sexless, almost bodiless Roderick Usher, dying without issue; of Hawthorne's eunuchoid voyeurs from Clifford Pyncheon to Miles Coverdale; of Melville's castrated hero-villain Ahab and his saintly impotents, Bartleby and Billy Budd; of Henry James's libido-less romantics from Christopher Newman to Lambert Strether, whose Happy Ending is *not* to get the girl; of T. S. Eliot's Gerontion and J. Alfred Prufrock, etc. etc.

To be sure, as early as Henry Miller, there were efforts to create a counterimage of the American hero as tireless cocksman. Moreover, not merely did Mailer and Bellow attempt, in their quite different ways, to follow his example but so also in theirs did Philip Roth and Jack Kerouac and countless others now forgotten. From the vantage point of the nineties, however, and in the entire context of our literature, all their efforts seem in mythic terms, if not quite un-American, at least eccentric or irrelevant. Certainly, none of their prepotent protagonists has come to possess our imaginations like the genital cripples and refugees from sex of our central tradition. Not Mailer's Sergius O'Shaughnessy or Stephen Rojack, surely, or even Roth's insatiable Portnoy, who is almost redeemed by his last-minute impotence in the land of his ancestors. Roth, as a matter of fact, despite his commitment to the Sexual Revolution, is drawn over and over into confessing the fear of phallic failure that lies just below his superficial bravado. Indeed, one of his most moving stories is the comic-pathetic "Epstein," whose aging anti-hero finds in the bed of a complaisant neighbor not the "apocalyptic orgasm" he is seeking but a heart attack.

Indeed, many practicing novelists in the last decades of the twentieth century—especially as they grow older—find it easier to identify with eunuchs than with studs. As I began to write this essay, for instance, there lay open on my desk Kurt Vonnegut's novel *End Game*, whose protagonist turns out to be—not unexpectedly—a "neutered pharmacist" called Otto Walz: a symbol (the author tells us in a defensive preface intended for critics like me) of his own "declining sexuality." Yet Vonnegut remains a favorite writer of young readers, as well as of the no-longer-young generation that first discovered him in the time of the Counter Culture, identifying even then with his earlier eunuchoid characters like Mr. Rosewater.

How could they not, since, though to one degree or another they actually lived the "sexual revolution" that Mailer preached, at a less conscious level they were possessed by the mythology of the Comic Books they had grown up reading behind their parents' backs. And at the heart of that mythology is Siegel and Shuster's "Man of Steel": an impotent savior of mankind who could never—either as Clark Kent or Superman—make it with Lois Lane. It is only that Super-Eunuch, perhaps, who has in this century achieved for the American mass audience the archetypal status of Rip or Huck; though for a smaller audience which still prefers words on the page to images on the screen, two characters created by Nobel Laureates have similarly escaped the texts in which they first appeared and come to live the free lives of myths.

I am referring, of course, to Hemingway's stoic castrato, Jake Barnes, and his dark shadow, Faulkner's emasculated voyeur and (with the aid of a corn cob) rapist, Popeye, whose name, of course, evokes once more the mythology of the Comics. But this seems fair enough in light of the fact that *Sanctuary*, in which he appears, borders on being shameless sensationalist schlock. It has consequently not only been regarded with suspicion by the guardians of High Culture; but the author himself felt obliged to apologize for it publicly—claiming that from the start he had intended it to be a pornographic potboiler: a way of making a quick buck by giving the mass audience a cheap masochistic thrill.

Whatever we think of it (and I esteem it very highly indeed), it would be foolish to deny that *Sanctuary* is basically an extended dirty joke in rather poor taste; yet it is something more or less, since the laughter stirred by its grotesque situations and caricatured dramatis personae is being constantly undercut by horror and revulsion. We tend to laugh anyhow, as we do at *any* story about someone who can't get it up and is obliged to get his kicks by peeping at someone else who can. Only thus can we exorcize the horror evoked by the suggestion implicit in such stories that a similar fate may await *us*—if we live so long. The darker and deeper wish/fear embodied in the image of impotent rape, however—along with its implied message that rape is a confession of the fear of impotence—is no laughing matter. And it is precisely its ability to take us thus beyond laughter that makes *Sanctuary* unequivocally American; different, at any rate, from the classic "dirty books" of Europe, whether they be grimly ironic like the Marquis de Sade's *Justine* or blithely good-humored like John Cleland's *Fanny Hill*.

To be sure, as we have already noticed, certain twentieth-century American writers have tried to naturalize such European "pornotopias," dreams of eternal youth and unflagging potency. But there is something deep in the American psyche (certainly, in my own) which finds profoundly alien all such fantasies of sex and sadism without responsibility or guilt. What appeals to us more is the model provided by Mark Twain's *1601, or A Fireside Conversation,* the sole piece of hard porn produced by a major writer of our own nineteenth century. Written in 1876, when Twain had just passed his fortieth birthday and was already beginning to create the myth of pregenital innocence which has haunted us ever since, it remained for a long time a secret even to many of his most ardent admirers. At first, indeed, he seems to have wanted it that way; distributing it only in letter form to a small group of close male friends—including a Protestant minister from Hartford, a poet from Buffalo, and a rabbi from Albany. And though he eventually had it printed (at West Point, of all places!), it was in a limited edition of fifty. Nonetheless, he is on record as having said it was one of the few pieces of his own at which he had ever laughed aloud; and he seems to have believed its early readers who tried to convince him that it was a minor masterpiece which should not be allowed to disappear.

Subsequent critics, however, have not concurred. Indeed, *1601* is scarcely mentioned in any "scholarly" studies to this very day; it is not even listed in the compendious bibliography of his work which appears in the third volume of *The Literary History of the United States*. Yet it repays hard reading, being essential not only to an understanding of Twain's own troubled attitudes toward sex but of the culture which produced him. Despite the fact that it is set in the court of Queen Elizabeth I and written in what he intended to be the colloquial British English of the seventeenth century, this presumable extract from the diary of "an old man who feels his nobility to be defiled by what he has to report" is prototypically American. And perhaps the most American thing about it is that though it is pornography, gross and explicit, it contains *no* fucking and sucking.

For the first ten of its fifteen pages in fact (except for a fascinating aside attributed to Sir Walter Raleigh, about how "in ye uttermost parts of America they copulate not until they be five and thirty years of age…and do it then but once in seven years"), it is almost purely scatological: a long discourse on farting. Then in its closing paragraph, without transition or motivation, it switches—becoming, in fact, a classic version of the myth of impotence and old age which I had set out to examine:

> Now was Sr. Walter minded of a tale…about a mayde, which being likely to suffer rape by an olde archbishoppe, did smartly contrive a device to save her mayden-

hedde, and said to him: "First, my lord, I prithee, take
out thy holy toole and piss before mee," which doing, lo!
his member felle, and wolde not rise again.

Superficially, the disastrous ending of *1601* (with its refrain,
"and wolde not rise again") resembles that of the Myth of the Dirty
Old Man. But this time around the *senex* is cheated of the inappropriate consummation he so shamelessly desires not by death
but by detumescence, and we are moved therefore through pathos
to laughter and beyond. And this is indeed something new: something peculiarly American, perhaps, as I have already suggested, as
well as peculiarly modern. The archetypal story which I examined
in my earlier meditation on the Dirty Old Man assumes that sexual desire and phallic potency (however unseemly they may be in
the aged) never cease as long as life lasts. Consequently, what is
presented as problematical is the propriety rather than the possibility of sex in the shadow of death. Twain's dirty little story, on the
other hand, represents a transitional stage on the way to the myth
behind the brochures of the sexpill hucksters who invade my privacy with each day's mail—in which the propriety of concupis-
cence at an advanced age is taken for granted, while its possibility
is assumed to be (without medical intervention) doubtful in the
extreme.

Truly, the fear of impotency seems to have grown rather than
diminished in direct proportion to our loss of any sense of sex as
sinful or shameful or indecorous. I am, however, by no means convinced that in the depths of our troubled psyches, even the most
enlightened and liberated among us are not moved still by the
guilts reflected in and reinforced by the Myth of the Dirty Old
Man. How hard we find it, for instance, not to snigger at public
displays of affection between crabbed age and youth, though we
have presumably learned to be ashamed of such titters and the
archaic guilts which prompt them. After all, we live in an era when
the Sexual Revolution has succeeded to a point where compulsory

one-night stands in youth and required mate swapping in middle age have come to seem the norms of bourgeois life. To be sure, like all revolutions, it, too, has failed; since neurosis and cancer, war and the profit motive have not disappeared as promised with the release of old repressions.

Nonetheless, psychologically we *have* changed, have we not, even those of us who have reached an age where it might well seem advisable to make a virtue of what will soon be a necessity—by abandoning the ultimately doomed pursuit of yet one more sexual climax, and one more beyond that. A wedge has driven between us and what was long considered wisdom. No longer can we really understand, much less sympathize with, the cry of relief of Sophocles, when at age eighty sexual desire finally ceased to trouble him: "At last I have been delivered from the harsh taskmaster." Similarly, the New Testament verse that reminds us that some have become eunuchs for the sake of the Kingdom of Heaven—and suggests that more of us should—dismays and repels us. And we are even more dismayed to learn what was long kept secret from the vulgar by his privileged acolytes, that Sigmund Freud himself (which is to say, the putative father of sexual liberation) gave up sex completely after reaching the age of forty. He did it, to be sure, in the name of secular sublimation rather than Christian chastity; but since for a long time now sublimation has become as dirty a word as its non-psychoanalytical equivalents: dignity and decorum and self-restraint. Under whatever name, we are through with the denial of the flesh forever, which is to say, for as long as life lasts.

Or so at least I used to think when I was young. At this point, however, I must confess that though the harsh taskmaster drives me still, I find it difficult, having come some fifteen thousand times in my life, to look forward to my fifteen thousand and first orgasm with the utopian hopefulness of youth; or for that matter, to contemplate the possibility of its being my last with the dismay of middle age. Thus also, having—coward that I am—already died a thousand deaths, I find I can entertain the notion of my own inevitable extinction with similar equanimity. And I am therefore able to believe that in some ultimate sense the two concomitants of aging, impotence and death, like the two myths which embody them, are inextricably bound together.

In any case, it has become possible for me at long last to imagine myself uttering—with whatever vestigial ambivalence—the Sophoclean sigh of post-erotic relief. I know now that from the start I must have *wished* for ultimate impotence quite as deeply as I feared it; even as I must have yearned for the final obliteration of consciousness as fervently as I dreaded it. Nor do I wish to be delivered to the dark side of my ambivalence in regard to either. Indeed, I suspect that if ever I became immune to the longing to be done living and loving, I could, to be sure, cast a colder eye on the ads for Corazine-DL and NSP-270; but I would also (and it is a price I will not pay) no longer be able to remember what had once seemed to me so heartbreakingly funny about Mark Twain's dirty little joke.

Child Abuse: An Amateur Approach

⇒€

THOUGH I DO NOT consider myself a professional in the field of "child abuse," in terms of lived experience rather than specialized learning, I feel I have as much right as any one else to speak on the subject. More right, indeed, than some; since not only have I been like everyone else, a child, but unlike many others, I am a parent as well. I have participated in the rearing of eight children, all of whom, I am quite willing to confess, I have on some occasions and to some degree "abused," as that slippery term is defined by one or another of the self-declared experts in the field. Moreover, as a child I was myself "abused" by my parents: harshly scolded, angrily whipped, rejected, teased, scorned—treated, in short, as less than fully human. Or at least so it seemed to me then. I can clearly remember telling myself in pain and tears, at age four or five, "Never forget. Never forget!"; and indeed I have not.

One of the reasons I became a writer was to share those memories of my childhood rage and grief with others who had repressed similar ones. My first published story dealt with the topic—which means, does it not, that I have never really doubted that the complex and difficult subject of violence in parent-child relationships comes within the purview of literature. Whether literature yields insights into the kind of questions asked by "professionals"—such as "Can child-rearing values be imposed on others?" or "Should society intervene in a family because of the likelihood that a child would be harmed?"—is quite another matter. Literature is more interested in framing new questions than in answering old ones. Nonetheless, long before social scientists had invented the term "child abuse," much less begun to discuss it candidly, cruelty to children, especially in its ultimate expression, infanticide, was the subject of playwrights and poets.

In Euripides' *Medea*, for instance, a mother driven out of her mind by jealousy of her husband kills her children, while the Chorus chants in shocked disapproval:

> O your heart must have been made of rock and steel,
> You who can kill
> With your own hand the fruit of your own womb...
> What horror more can be? O women's love,
> So full of trouble,
> How many evils you have caused already.

Such scenes are rare in Classical Drama, though the practice of infanticide by exposure was common enough in the Ancient World, where it constituted a form of "population control," regarded not without terror though finally accepted. But the poets and playwrights of antiquity typically do not let such exposed children die and portray them instead as having been somehow miraculously preserved.

Nearly two thousand years later, Shakespeare in *The Winter's Tale* seems to have been bound still by that same convention. Though Leontes, the jealous King of his play, is at first resolved to kill the girl-child he falsely considers illegitimate, she survives to preside over the play's Happy Ending. His son, Manilius, it is true, does die but *not* at his father's hand. Instead, he pines away in supersensitive response to his father's displeasure and his mother's dishonor. Most readers, however, remember the plight of neither of these children as vividly as they do the purely hypothetical murder of an anonymous child whom Lady Macbeth evokes in the context of weaning, which is to say, the inevitable act of maternal rejection:

...I have given suck, and know
How tender 'tis to love the babe that milks me:
I would, wile it was smiling in my face,
Have plucked my nipple from his boneless gums,
And dashed his brains out, had I so sworn as you
Have done to this...

In any case mothers are the mythological perpetrators-in-chief of one of the two extreme forms of child abuse, infanticide (the other being child rape, whose perpetrator is mythologically the father). Modern researchers tell us that, in fact, the majority of infants killed in the home do die at the hands of their mothers. We now tend, however, to see such murderers of their offspring not as strong-minded heroine-villains, like Medea and Lady Macbeth but like Goethe's seduced and abandoned Gretchen; which is to say, a victim as pitiful as the newborn child whom she drowns before killing herself. Nonetheless, even after the triumph of Sentimentalism in the Age of Nobody's-Fault, it is still women who are typically shown murdering their own children.

The Bible, however, portrays such killers of helpless infants as patriarchal rather than matriarchal; its key images being the Slaughter of the Innocents and the Sacrifice of Isaac. The Slaughter of the Innocents is, in fact, told twice over, the first time attributed to the Egyptian Pharaoh and the second to King Herod; but both of these murders are perpetrated by hostile rulers rather than heartless fathers who order wholesale holocausts for political rather than personal reasons. In the case of Abraham and Isaac, of course, it is an actual Father who is portrayed as threatening the life of his single son; but the knife he raises is never permitted to fall. Moreover, the Rabbis have always taught that Isaac was a consenting adult—his age at the moment he was bound to the altar being thirty. Christian painters, however, have usually limned him as a helpless child, or even, influenced perhaps by the iconography of the Circumcision of Jesus on the eighth day after his birth, an infant. Indeed, for many centuries the presumed anniversary of that event on January first was celebrated by the Church as a children's festival. And though there are present-day writers on child abuse who regard circumcision as gratuitous cruelty, the Church Fathers, like the Rabbis, thought of it as commemorating the end of ritual infanticide, as the bloody Mother Cults of the Ancient Near East were being replaced by the benign patriarchal Cult of Jehovah.

In any case, the works to which I have alluded so far seem to me to cast light on *why* the "battered child" remained for so long "invisible" to the workers in hospitals where such children were often sent to die. Not until 1945 did Dr. John Caffey of Columbia University publish a paper, tentatively identifying the "syndrome" he had observed in patients at the Babies Hospital in New York City, characterized by "(1) tender swelling deep in the soft tissues; (2) cortical thickenings in the skeleton; and (3) onset during the first three months of life…" as a condition produced by "intentional ill-treatment of the infant." And it was 1962 before any physician forthrightly described "the battered child syndrome" in a journal intended for circulation outside of a tiny group of specialists. But *why* did doctors and nurses not earlier see—know how to see, permit themselves to see—what was before them day after day after day? It is clearly not a matter of the inadequacy of the techniques, but of a climate of expectation, an a priori set of assumptions about what was conceivable in parent-child relationships.

Such assumptions were typically derived not from medical textbooks but from the novels doctors read, the plays and movies and TV shows they watched from childhood on. They fall, therefore, within the purview of professional writers and professional readers, which is to say, literary critics. Poets, playwrights, and novelists are accustomed to thinking of social reality not as given but as determined by perception; and so they have an advantage over physicians, surgeons, and, indeed, all social scientists with a strong behavioral bias. Consequently, they have no difficulty in understanding not just why "abused children" remained for so long invisible to medical professionals, but why all children, why "the Child," remained for so long unnoticed, unperceived by *everyone*; and why when he did finally appear he entered the scene battered and weeping? *The Invisible Man*, the title of a novel by Ralph Ellison which appeared in 1952 provides a clue, suggesting that all maximally excluded and exploited groups in society, all "niggers," whatever their skin color, tend to be thrust into a limbo of the unnoticed by their oppressors, from which the victims must be delivered before we can become aware of their suffering, much less strive to ameliorate it. That job was done for children by certain imaginative writers of the nineteenth century, who modified the sensibility of their age, teaching adults to weep over the plight of the young, even though they'd had not yet ceased to flog them at home and at school.

However, ever since the publication of *Oliver Twist* (the first book by a respected author to make a suffering child its protagonist), the mind of the West has been split down the middle on the subject of corporal punishment of children—some advocating its complete abolition, some wholeheartedly defending it. Most of us, though, manage to have our cake and eat it, too: either walloping our kids and living to regret it, or sparing the rod (at the cost of ulcers arising from repressed anger), then blaming ourselves when they fail our hopes and expectations. Or, in cases where the division runs right down the middle of our own heads, we tend to regress to the Victorian state of shamelessly weeping over the plight of children whom we shamefully abuse.

The latter is a disconcerting thought, pointing as it does to a widespread sentimental duplicity of which I cannot declare myself totally innocent. But this is, perhaps, because I have been much influenced by Sigmund Freud's disturbing essay "A Child Is Being Beaten." First published in 1919, it describes a masturbatory fantasy shared by a number of Freud's patients (themselves from well-to-do and enlightened families in which beating was rare and never brutal) of an anonymous, genderless child being flogged by an indistinct, unidentified adult; the dreamer, ostensibly, present only as an observer, witness, or voyeur. Such fantasies are, Freud points out, typically kept alive by fiction. "In my patient's *milieu* it was almost always books whose contents gave a new stimulus," he writes, "to the beating-phantasies; those accessible to young people, such as...*Uncle Tom's Cabin*, etc."

If such books can thus penetrate the depths of the individual Unconscious, surely they can penetrate the Collective Unconscious as well, determining the way in which a given community perceives, judges, and reacts to child punishment in general. At any rate, by analyzing the Cult of the Battered Child in nineteenth-century fiction, as well as its roots in the eighteenth century and the Fairy Tales much admired then, I hope to lend a new perspective to what happened in the mid-twentieth century when such insights moved from the realm of literature to that of "science," motivating new trends in medical care and social action.

In order to understand better the historical context in which such developments occurred, however, I have also consulted non-literary "authorities" on the subject, beginning with Lloyd De Mause, a psycho-sociologist who had been a student of mine some years before in a course in which I had tried to demonstrate how literature can be a source of insight into general culture. I was disconcerted to find him, in an essay called "The Evolution of Childhood," dismissing literature as a source of reliable information about child rearing. "The literary historians," he writes, "mistaking books for life, construct a fictional picture of childhood, as though one could know what really happened in the nineteenth-century American home by reading *Tom Sawyer*."

What he had forgotten by the time he came to write his study in 1974 (or what perhaps he had never believed) is that literature can tell us how people at a given historical moment perceive and evaluate and therefore *experience* what they are doing. Poets and novelists reflect, reinforce—sometimes even slowly but perceptibly *change*—awareness and attitudes, which is all the "historical reality" available to those who live after them, maybe all the "historical reality" there ever was. To be sure, imaginative writers do not accumulate statistics like the social scientist. Nor do they generalize discursively like the philosopher, much less describe particular cases like the historian or journalist. What they register in narrative and image is at once singular and inclusive, what Hegel calls a "concrete universal" and I prefer to think of as an "archetype" or "myth": the perceptual-conceptual grid through which a period, a national culture, a class, sex, or generation first "sees," then makes sense of, the life it lives on both the conscious and unconscious level.

Clearly, then, in order to understand not merely what at any historical juncture adults objectively did to children (flogged them or did not; had sex with them or made them erotically taboo; carefully preserved their lives or killed them), but what such action or inaction subjectively signified, we need to know what were the reigning Myths of the Child, the Parent, Authority, Violence, Law, Love, and Death. We must, moreover, be similarly aware of what for *us* are the corresponding major Myths, lest we remain time-bound ethnocentrists, judging the child-bearing practices of other places and times by our own consciously avowed or unconsciously maintained standards.

If we are so aware we are unlikely to be tempted into unequivocally maligning the past and congratulating ourselves, as De Mause does when he writes

> ...the further back one goes in history, the less effective parents are in meeting the developing needs of the child...if today in America there are less than a million abused children, there would be a point back in history where most children were what we now consider abused.

Insofar as modern sensibility and the modern Myth of the Child have extended the range of tabooed violence between parents and children to include everything from swaddling and circumcision to telling blood-curdling stories in the nursery, the past can be viewed as a Chamber of Horrors. But in terms of the treatment parents inflict or permit to be inflicted on their children which they themselves consider "abuse," it can be argued the present represents a fall from a relatively idyllic past.

The beginnings of this "fall" to a place in which a wider and wider wedge is driven between child-rearing behavior and the values by which it is contemporaneously judged (so that corporal punishment, for instance—not to mention infanticide and the sexual violation of children—is on the one hand drastically restricted, and on the other hand, more and more guilt-ridden when it does happen) can best be traced, I believe, in the kind of nineteenth-century books about children and their parents to which I alluded earlier, particularly some novels of Charles Dickens. Even a cursory examination will show how child rearing in our time is characterized not merely by a conflict between theory and practice, but by a discrepancy between what each of us would like to believe we believe on this score and what it turns out under stress we really do believe, as a result of the persistence in our deep psyches of attitudes we have inherited from the recent or remote past.

It should be remembered that when Dickens's *Oliver Twist* (1838), *Nicholas Nickleby* (1839), and *David Copperfield* (1850)—in all of which the corporal punishment of children is portrayed as vicious abuse—first appeared, most of his readers were still also reading the Bible, in which the use of the rod is enjoined rather than forbidden. Moreover, even now a favored generation of middle-class whites practicing behavior recommended by the latest "permissive" guides to child rearing, are likely to have had grandparents still committed to that orthodox doctrine about child discipline. Moreover, they live in a world where certain of their neighbors still believe that their offspring must be chastened not just with words but the lash, in order to "break their wills," since, as St. Augustine put it, "the innocence of children is more a matter of weakness of the limbs than purity of the heart."

If some children once died under the lash (as some born to the orthodox of various faiths do even now), it could be attributed to "the Will of God"; and, in any case, it seemed less reprehensible, less remarkable even, in a time of large families and high infant mortality caused not only by accident and disease but by such accepted forms of deliberate, or subintended infanticide as the "farming out" of babies to "angel-makers," who doped them with opiates and let them die. Objectively speaking, both beating and "farming out" constituted a kind of unconscious "population control," like the much earlier ritualized practices of Exposure or Child Sacrifice or ritual Maiming. But like them, too, *subjectively* speaking, these practices permitted a socially acceptable discharge of the hostility inevitably engendered in parents by the birth of a child.

We scarcely need the evidence of literature to persuade us of the new parent's sense of the circumscription of freedom, the sometimes almost unendurable increase of responsibility ("He who has a child," Jonathan Swift once remarked, "has given a hostage to fortune"), as well as the appearance of a rival for the spouse's affection, and a harbinger of old age and the disappearance of vigor and beauty; not to mention the added drain on a family's resources and living space, especially exacerbated in the case of the poor. It is not easy for parents to admit that they hate and resent as well as love and cherish their own offspring, any more than it is for them to confess that sometimes their love (particularly for children of the opposite sex) crosses over the line of erotic desire, threatening, perhaps even breaking, the incest taboo.

It is even harder for them to grant that their children hate and resent and lust for them, as Freud scandalized the world by suggesting. But this doubleness of feeling between parent and child was on literary record centuries before Freud—registered with especial sensitivity and nakedness in the "fairy tales" to which almost all of us have been exposed. First written down in the late seventeenth century, such stories reinforce as well as reveal our primal ambivalence. Their essential subject is, in fact, what we have come to call "child abuse" and "child molestation" and the psychological roots of these: the father's lust for and the mother's murderous jealousy of the daughter; and the son's dream of delivering by patricide his mother (as well as himself) from the real or presumed tyranny of the father.

To be sure, fairy tales typically encrypt these fantasies by representing the Bad Father, i.e, everything the child hates and fears in his own male parent, as a Giant or Ogre, usually cannibalistic; while the Bad Mother, the parent who, after bearing and suckling them, refuses the breast or seems to prefer the father, is figured forth as a Stepmother or a Witch. Sometimes, indeed, she assumes the personae of *both* in the same story—as in *Hansel and Gretel*. In that tale, the Good Mother, the nurturing and loving female parent, is present only as a posthumous memory, dead presumably ever since her children's infancy; as if, indeed, the only wholly good mother were a dead mother.

Such "splitting" or "doubling" in fantasy, at the behest of our ambivalence, of characters single in real life is familiar to us from our own dreams; and it is easy enough therefore to decode not only the Witch whom Hansel and Gretel deceive and destroy, but the Giant whom Jack kills to ensure his Happy Ending. It is worth reflecting for a little while on the fact that the Happy Endings of Fairy Tales most often involve not just an escape and/or marriage—i.e., an assurance that despite parental abuse, children will survive to grow up and have children of their own—but the incredibly brutal punishment of the Bad Parent surrogate.

The Ogress, for instance, who tries to kill Sleeping Beauty after she has been awakened and wed in the version of the story published by Charles Perrault, ends up eaten alive by a vat-full of vipers, serpents, and poisonous toads; while in the Grimm Brothers' especially atrocious "The Juniper Tree," the evil woman who killed her stepson and fed him to his father in the form of a blood pudding is crushed to death by a millstone; and in "Snow

White," the foiled, wicked stepmother is forced to dance in red-hot iron shoes until she drops dead.

In each of these tales, the grandmothers and nannies, who seem originally to have told them, satisfy with fantasies of bloody revenge both their own resentment against their grown children and their grandchildren's desire for revenge against their parents, who are, of course, the same people. In no fairy tales, in any case, are children portrayed as innocent, long-suffering and all-forgiving. Indeed, there are some Old Wives' Tales which call on us to rejoice in the destruction of bad boys or girls. Sometimes such children are portrayed as being downright wicked, but often they are merely heedless of parental injunctions, like Goldilocks in "The Three Bears" or Little Red Ridinghood, who in the earliest versions of her story is eaten by the Wolf, rather than being delivered to a kind of second birth in a Caesarian section administered by the good patriarchal figure of the Woodcutter. The repressed dark impulses we have been examining are exorcised by such tales; and a similar cathartic function is performed by corporal punishment, as long as it is expected/accepted by children themselves and condoned by the official guardians of value, lay and ecclesiastical.

Moreover, as long as such conditions prevail and the Myths on which they are based go unchallenged, no new guilts are created that would be even more psychologically disabling than the ones such behavior sought to exorcise. But beginning somewhere late in the eighteenth century, occurred two Psychic Revolutions simultaneously: a redefinition of childhood and a rejection of violence as a way of solving social problems. The first is part of a larger movement called "Primitivism." Associated with the names of Jean-Jacques Rousseau, William Blake, and William Wordsworth, that radical shift reversed many traditional values, prizing the Savage more than the Civilized, the Female more than the Male, Blacks more than Whites, Impulse more than Reason, the Unconscious more than the Conscious, the Child more than the Adult. The second began with an attack on Capital Punishment and eventuated in Pacifism, the disavowal of War. But there are paradoxes implicit in all this. One of the chief early opponents of Capital Punishment, for instance, was the Marquis de Sade, whom ironically we remember for that eroticizing of violence called "Sadism." And the teachings of Rousseau, first laureate of the Child, were cited by apologists for the French Revolution and the Terror, the model for the series of bloody revolts of the oppressed that, along with Total Warfare, have characterized the ensuing age.

For our purposes, however, the most interesting and relevant manifestation of the revulsion against violence was the widespread Fear of Flogging, which eventuated in an impassioned attack on the hitherto accepted beating of animals, Black slaves, schoolboys, enlisted men, wives, and little children. Oddly enough, it began with a protest against the mistreatment of horses and dogs, then was transferred to humans. Indeed, the first prosecution of batterers of children was conducted under the laws passed at the instigation of the Society for the Prevention of Cruelty to Animals. But in fiction, all the insulted and injured became subjects of concern.

Harriet Beecher Stowe, for instance, had excoriated the flogging of slaves in *Uncle Tom's Cabin*, Herman Melville that of sailors in *Billy Budd*, while Charles Dickens specialized in women and children: he began with wife beating in *The Pickwick Papers*, then passed on to the caning of boys in *Oliver Twist*, *Nicholas Nickleby*, and *David Copperfield*. The beating of small boys by their schoolmasters in particular remained a major theme of Kipling's *Stalky and Co* and Mark Twain's *Tom Sawyer*. But girls (though beaten in life and in sado-masochistic pornography addressed primarily to men) seem to have preferred to have their plight represented through surrogates, particularly horses.

Even today, for instance, they seem to respond passionately to Anna Sewell's *Black Beauty*, in which Miss Sewell speaks not just for but in the voice of a battered horse. A lesser writer than other laureates of the Fear of Flogging, she won with her small, sentimental masterpiece (the only book she ever wrote) the hearts first of Victorian reformers (the SPCA distributed her novel), then of the children, who apparently identified with her whipped, starved, but once sleek and beautiful beasts of burden. What remains implicit in such works becomes explicit in Charles Dickens.

In his *David Copperfield* he describes the double indignity of being beaten in a world where even to the child himself the mere fact of having been flogged is proof of his guilt. "Mr. Murdstone! Sir!" David cries to his stepfather, whom he had earlier watched "binding something round the bottom of...a lithe and limber cane." "Don't! Pray don't beat me!" And our sympathy secured, he continues:

> He had my head as in a vice, but I twined round him somehow, and stopped him for a moment, entreating him not to beat me. It was only a moment that I stopped him, for he cut me heavily an instant afterwards, and in the same instant I caught the hand with which he held me in my mouth, between my teeth, and bit it through. It sets my teeth on edge to think of it.
>
> He beat me then, as if he would have beaten me to death...Then he was gone; and the door was locked outside; and I was lying, fevered and hot, and torn, and sore, and raging in my puny way, upon the floor.
>
> How well I recollect, when I became quiet, what an unnatural stillness seemed to reign through the whole house! How well I remember, when my smart and passion began to cool, how wicked I began to feel!
>
> I sat listening for a long while, but there was not a sound. I crawled up from the floor, and saw my face in the glass, so swollen, red, and ugly that it almost frightened me. My strips were sore and stiff, and made me cry afresh, when I moved; but they were nothing to the guilt I felt...

In any case, David is finally seen as the guileless and guiltless victim (we, as readers, not being permitted to share his self-condemnation): a Child, in short, perceived through the haze of the Rousseauistic myth of original innocence, rather than a Limb of Satan, perceived through the grid of Orthodox Christianity. Many of the victimized children in Dickens manage to die; as do the poor little boys, some of them actually rich, along with the saintly little girls destroyed by adult lust and greed, who appear in the pages of *Oliver Twist, Nicholas Nickleby, The Old Curiosity Shop, Dombey and Son, Hard Times,* "A Christmas Carol," etc, etc., are portrayed finally as Little Angels, too good for a world whose cruelty to them reveals its essential corruption.

Dickens was the first to bring together for the general reader the Fear of Flogging and the Cult of the Innocent Child—a formidable combination, useful for those whose trade was tugging at the heartstrings. Unwilling as yet to give up completely the kinds of behavior he attacked and unable to turn what was formerly a public virtue into a private vice, his audience felt guilty when they practiced on their children forms of discipline which their parents had visited upon them without self-reproach. This guilt Dickens permitted them to exorcise in tears; though at the same time he *compounded* it, by reinforcing a mythic version of childish innocence completely at odds with the actual behavior of their own sons and daughters: the willfulness, sullenness, and irrational aggression which had probably driven them, in the first instance, to pick up the cane or the switch.

Dickens was not unaware that children (of whom he had ten) could behave badly on occasion. Indeed, the two boys who appear in his first book, *The Pickwick Papers,* are presented as comic monsters. One, called simply "The Fat Boy," is a tub of guts, indolent to the point of catatonia, but in his few waking moments sly, lustful, and given to scaring the wits out of anyone near him; while the other, identified only as the son of Mr. Pickwick's cunning housekeeper, Mrs. Bardle, enters the scene kicking, pinching, and punching that kindly old gentleman. And even as late as *The Old Curiosity Shop,* there is Quilp's young apprentice, an ugly and ill-tempered lad, continually thrashed by his master: that grotesque, dwarfish abuser of his own wife whom Dickens once ironically remarked was the closest thing to a self-portrait in his entire opus, to whom he is endlessly insolent: the two bound together by a pathological bond of hate and dependency.

Such demonic children are seldom remembered by Dickens-lovers, yet they represent the beginnings of a counter-tradition of child portraiture which has persisted well up into our own time. Examples range from Mark Twain's *Tom Sawyer* and *Huckleberry Finn* to the once-famous *Peck's Bad Boy*, Booth Tarkington's *Penrod and Sam* and the little menace of O. Henry's much anthologized "The Ransom of the Red Chief," as well as comic-strip characters like Hans and Fritz, the infamous Katzenjammer Kids, whose sadistic pranks were invariably climaxed by even more sadistic punishments. Such avatars of the Bad Boy usually turn out to have hearts of gold, and in any case they do nothing really atrocious. But even when they pass over the line separating them from what we call in the jargon of our own time "juvenile delinquents"—i.e., criminals below the age of responsibility as defined by law—we are likely to be laughing too hard to notice.

Huck Finn—America's favorite freckle-faced kid—is, for instance, thought of as ultimately lovable and even "innocent," though at one point he is quite ready to shoot dead his drunk and threatening "Pap." As a matter of fact, "Pap" is finally murdered to insure the book's strange Happy Ending, but he dies offstage at other hands, leaving Huck guilty only of playing hooky, lying, petty theft, grand larceny, and vagrancy, free to run away from home once more. Yet running away from home was seen in earlier books (written when writers worried more about parent abuse than child abuse) as a heinous crime: the equivalent on the child's part to abandonment on the part of his father and mother.

It can be argued that in the past Americans were more tolerant of Bad Boys than they have since become. For a while, at least, society permitted (in some sense, encouraged) real boys to play

the Katzenjammer role, as a kind of training in machismo—
though, to be sure, not without brutal corporal punishment that
constituted a complementary part of that same training and a clear
understanding that in adolescence their sadistic pranks would be
left behind. Occasionally such privileged pranksters turned out to
be "Bad Bad boys," who, like Billy the Kid, never outgrew their
"mischievousness," ending in jail or hanged or shot. Most, however, only turned out to be only "Good Bad Boys," becoming finally
solid and useful citizens. But all of them, from age nine to fourteen, acted out with the cooperation of their spanking fathers, a
semi-ritualized oedipal conflict. "The Revolt of the Young Bulls…a
sort of guerilla warfare against their oppressors," Clyde Brion
Davis calls it in an illuminating essay on the subject, included in
his book *The Age of Indiscretion.*

Sometime just before World War II, what had been tolerated as
"mischief" and shrugged off with the observation that "boys will be
boys" began to be stigmatized as "criminal," even as the strict
paternal discipline which had answered it in kind began to be
regarded as "abuse." For a while it was not totally banned but
restricted to certain festivals of release, particularly Halloween. In
my own lifetime, however, even that licensed annual riot, renamed
"trick or treat," became almost exclusively a quest for sweets, a
kind of licensed begging, with only the vestigial threat of violence
(punishable by law if it went out of control) rather than a privileged release of hostility.

Since the end of World War II, such a release has been available to well-brought-up children only vicariously, in the popular
arts. Hans and Fritz, for instance, still torment *der* Captain and *die*
Mama and *der* Inspector in a comic strip renamed *The Captain
and the Kids*; but they no longer seem either role models or reflections of action life. And Walt Disney has distanced his fables of
oedipal violence even more by representing humans as animals.
Television, it is true, manages—especially in nighttime cop shows
(theoretically out of the child's viewing hours, so that just seeing

them is already an infringement of parental taboos)—to render with a kind of realism not just inter-generational guerilla warfare but the whole gamut of violent response otherwise driven underground in the bourgeois world.

It does this by setting such action in the "street," the alien world of the poor, where physical violence has remained an accepted way of settling all conflicts. In that world, it is practiced by wives against husbands, husbands against wives, children against parents, parents against children, teachers against students, students against teachers, criminals against cops, cops against criminals, brother against brother, neighbor against neighbor. In certain "integrated" public schools, where students from "good" neighborhoods and "bad" mingle, it erupts into class warfare, in which poor kids, raised by the rod and the bash in the head, harass, harry, blackmail, rob, and rough up richer kids, taught by their loving and forebearing parents to fear and eschew physical force.

Confronted by the eruption of violence in the world of childhood, the rich, the favored and the "enlightened" in frustration and bafflement call for aid from the "law" to which they have surrendered the use of force: sending in first social workers and then the cops. It is not merely their own children they seek thus to protect, they assure anyone who will listen, but the child persecutors as well, who—in light of their own mythologies—they believe even more ultimate victims. Brought up in what, according to genteel bourgeois standards, seems disorder and filth, fed irregularly and in contempt of "sane dietary principles," exposed too early to sex, drink, and drugs, then brutally beaten when they irk the parents who have neglected them, such kids inevitably practice the abuse visited on them, first on their weaker playmates, and then on their own kids.

Clearly, the only way out is somehow to impose on their parents the newer, gentler modes of child rearing, or when this does not work, turn the children over to foster parents already committed to such modes. Such attempts are, however, regarded as condescending or arrogant interventions not only by the "abusing" parents but sometimes by the "abused" children themselves. Meanwhile, the children of the bourgeois "do-gooders" aggravate the problem even further by emulating the lifestyles of the abused and violent children of the poor, using or selling drugs and running away from their sane and sheltered homes to make a life on the streets.

What they are in effect doing is rejecting the definition of themselves not just as "innocent" but as "children." The poetry and prose of the "Beats" and the "Hippies" makes clear that the intergenerational conflict of the fifties and sixties, the so-called Counter Culture, represented a second stage of the "guerilla warfare" of preteens against their "oppressors," who though they no longer "abuse" them physically, deny them their full humanity by imposing on them stereotypes of the child derived from the myth first invented in the eighteenth century, long after they are mature enough to bear children of their own in postindustrialized societies where menarche comes earlier and earlier.

It is, therefore, with the abuse of children at the upper limits of what used to be called "childhood," boys and girls between nine or ten and fourteen or fifteen, that the "enlightened" opponents of child abuse have most difficulty in coming to terms. Our laws still insist on those traditional limits, sixteen being the school-leaving age, eighteen that for voting, joining the armed forces, drinking hard liquor, and so on. But everywhere at this moment, there is a movement for more stringent punishment of juvenile offenders. Moreover, for some time now, first in the art novel, then in popular movies and TV shows, a new myth of the Non-innocent Child has emerged—not jocular and condescending portraits of the Naughty Prankster or the Bad Boy with a Heart of Gold, but scared and angry portrayals of the Demon Child. Henry James's pioneering *The Turn of the Screw*, an eerie tale of corrupted and corrupting children, before the turn of the century, followed fifty years later by the publication of Richard Hughe's *High Wind in Jamaica* and William Golding's immensely popular *The Lord of the Flies*. In them boys and girls are presented as responsible free agents who deliberately choose evil, reinventing on their own all the horrors of society, which according to Dickens is a conspiracy against what is purest and best in their unspoiled selves.

All three have been made into movies; and they have been followed by a series of films that includes *The Bad Seed, The Exorcist,* and *Carrie,* in which the satanism implicit in the them from the start has grown ever more explicit and the Child as Angel turns Child as Devil. A similar nightmare evocation of childish non-innocence in the world since Hitler has been projected in Jerry Kosinski's *The Painted Bird.* Meanwhile, certain cop shows have attempted to deal less fantastically with the reality behind the myth: the ten-year-old dope peddler and junkie, the twelve-year-old murderer and gun salesman of "Saturday Night Specials." Such shows also betray the rage of parents at their children's refusal to be what Rousseau, Wordsworth, Dickens, James Barrie, and Louisa May Alcott (new versions of those books also continue to make it on the tube) insist that they are or ought to be.

In the 1970s, at a point when the mounting campaign against violence on television (a campaign based on the notion of childhood innocence) was focusing on those very cop shows, they were beginning to work to death a scenario about virtuous mothers and their delinquent subteen or barely teenage sons. At first skeptical and defensive, such mothers become gradually aware that their sons are in fact the criminals that the street-wise detective hero has called them: a menace to society in general and to other children in particular. And at this point, such mothers "blow the whistle," sending their delinquent offspring off to jail—or, in one case at least, actually shooting the boy down with the gun that had belonged to his father. It is a cathartic denouement, vicariously fulfilling the threat of millions of parents, usually only whispered in the darkness of our heads when confronted by an "un-natural" child: "Christ, I'd like to kill the little bastard!" or "He'd be better off dead." For most of us, such vicarious fulfillment is enough; though the fact that we demand it of a popular art form (which we then self-righteously condemn) reveals the discrepancy between the life we live as parents and the outmoded mythology through which we try to make sense of it.

The murder of infants and preschoolers seems, on the face of it, much less problematical for believers in the myth of childhood innocence. It is rather the myth of motherly love that it challenges; since it is—as we have already observed—a crime perpetrated by mothers who, usually though not invariably, come from underprivileged households. Sometimes they are themselves teenagers without a mate, sometimes mature women conjugally abused or abandoned; in either case, often alcoholic or drug addicts. For them at any rate, infanticide constitutes a kind of postpartum birth control—the only kind possible indeed to those of them either invincibly ignorant or forbidden by their religion to practice sterilization, contraception, or abortion.

Ironically enough, most of those who criticize such ultimate child abuse, though they oppose various other kinds of violence, including capital punishment and war itself, are passionate advocates of abortion. It is not a matter of witting hypocrisy on their part, any more than it is for the antiabortionist "right-to-lifers" to defend the restoration of the death penalty. It would seem rather that almost all of us are driven to search desperately, below the level of full consciousness, for a myth system which will permit the ritualized slaughter of some human beings, actual or potential, who, according to that mythology, *do not really count*—whether these be fetuses, newborn infants, children, or hardened criminals of any age.

The testimony of the imaginative literature that I have examined would seem to indicate that for our psychic health it is necessary to reinstitute some form of permitted and ritualized "abuse" of the young and thus to keep within limits that stop short of maiming and murder the discharge of those inevitable hostilities that grow up between the generations. Indeed, at this very moment in certain states of Muslim North Africa and the Middle East, institutionalized flogging is being restored even for adult offenders, just as in presumably Christian capitalist America the death penalty has come back into favor. In general, it can be said the Cult of Antiviolence is dying everywhere in our terror-ridden world, along with the Rousseauistic myth of the child; and that we, particularly the most liberal and advanced thinkers among us, are caught in a No Man's Land between a moribund old myth system and a new one still struggling to be born.

In the interim, we must try to mediate as best we can our psychic dilemma: the ever more intolerable discrepancy between what all of us secretly suspect children are and what a few of us still feel obliged to pretend we believe them to be; as well as that between the child-rearing behavior we advocate and what we secretly wish we had nerve enough to practice even if we do not actually practice it. The most successful instrument for such mediation is the vicarious release of literature: including not just the kind of imaginative fiction I have been analyzing, but the sort of essay that I am about to conclude. I do not mean to accuse myself of being a pornographer in scholar's clothing. But I do feel moved to observe that such presumably "objective" studies as this one permit us, in the guise of condemning deviant, psychopathic, or criminal behavior, to evoke bloody images of child mayhem and slaughter that indulge and satisfy longings otherwise unconfessable by the "enlightened."

Images of the Doctor

in Literature and the Popular Arts

⊰≪⊱

EVEN THE MOST CASUAL watcher of TV dramas cannot help being aware of the omnipresence of medical personnel in those mythic re-creations of the lives we live, or at least would like to believe we live. Certainly, in the daytime serials, the "soaps" that preempt the Tube from noontime to dusk, physicians and surgeons, nurses and candy-stripers make up a disproportionate percentage of the dramatis personae. Indeed, after the living room and bedroom, the hospital room is the favorite setting for such immensely popular shows, one of the most popular of which is actually called *General Hospital.*

Nor does the situation change much when the sun goes down. Though in "prime time" Cops and Private Eyes tend to take center stage, nurses and doctors have also continued to play major roles in such favorite shows as *Marcus Welby, M.D., Quincy, M*A*S*H,* and *St. Elsewhere.* At the present moment, indeed, the hospital-based *E.R.* is the most watched drama on nighttime TV, with *Chicago Hope* not far behind.

In any case, the medical professionals in almost all such shows, daytime or nighttime, are presented favorably, positively: as caring, supportive, dedicated, and competent; which is to say, as good Fathers, kindly Uncles, or staunch Big Brothers—plus, of course, in response to feminist pressures, equally admirable Mothers, Aunts, and Big Sisters. When evil exists in hospital or sick bay as imagined on TV, it is likely to be attributed to corrupt administrators, civilian or military.

But this is precisely what we should have expected, is it not, in a society where we have grown more dependent on doctors than ever before in human history and where we reward them well for, presumably, a job well done! Yet such dependency characteristically breeds resentment as well as gratitude, especially when it becomes—for many of us at least—excessive, almost total. We insist these days that doctors be present in our schools and at our workplaces, and we would even hesitate to sail on a cruise ship or send our children to a summer camp without a physician in attendance. Moreover, we tend to put ourselves in their hands not just in times of crisis: more and more often we seek them out routinely, almost ritually, marking each stage of life's way from infancy to senility by some appropriate injection or vaccination, test, or change of medication.

Doctors have even come to preside over certain rites of passage once considered sacred: the white-coated intern, for instance, circumcising male neonates in place of the Shaman or *Moel*. So, too, they have preempted the duties of the midwife and the layer-out of the dead. Many of us, therefore, are likely to breathe our last without the presence of a priest; but almost none of us without a physician to certify that we are really, legally defunct—or, if we are rich enough to afford it, to prolong our existence. In this sense, the M.D. in the ICU becomes, as it were, not merely the servant of some reigning God, but a kind of a god himself, granting us an ersatz immortality with life support systems or organ transplants or (we begin to dream) cryogenic preservation of our bodies. And this seems fair enough in light of the fact that it may well have been another doctor who made the decision that allowed us to live in the first place: providing or not providing us with whatever was necessary to sustain our first few days of life on the basis of whether or not he judged us "viable" at birth.

Finally, the formerly sacrosanct rites of the confessional have also been transferred to the medical clinic. Even to general practitioners, obstetricians, and gynecologists, we are likely to confide—in the name of helping to complete our "case histories"—

secrets once reserved for the ear of an unseen, anonymous priest. And such secular confessions are, of course, essential to the practice of psychiatry: the cure of sick souls by the removal of guilt (once known as "absolution") and the deliverance of the patient from delusions bred by that guilt (formerly called "the casting out of demons"). Our modern exorcists, to be sure, no longer come to us, as was their wont, ceremoniously painted and in animal masks or bearing bell, book, and canon. Nor do they promise to heal us in the name of the divinities who have presumably created us. Instead, they invoke the spirit of godless "science"—in which alone most of us have what used to be called "faith."

Nonetheless, we regard such secular practitioners with the same mingling of reverence and awe, horror and resentment (the reverence and awe openly confessed, the horror and resentment secretly endured) with which our ancestors regarded the wonder-working servants of deities in whom we no longer believe we believe. Moreover, the archaic horror and resentment we feel toward the new healers is exacerbated rather than mitigated by the fact that they have demystified and desacralized not merely (like astronomers and geologists) the heavens and the earth but our very bodies as well, including what we once called our "hearts" (which we now know to be merely pumps, replaceable by a machine) and our "souls" (which we begin to suspect are no more than the sum total of electric and chemical impulses explicable in physiological terms).

All this is offensive enough to our traditional sense of ourselves and our essential humanity. But the final offense, perhaps, lies in the psychiatrists' subversion of the notion of "free will": their claim that by depth analysis, hypnosis, psycho-chemistry, or behavior modification, it is possible to control the patient's choice between what we have long thought of as "good" and "evil," even between life and death. To be sure, therapists of the spirit have had no greater rate of success in "curing" the ills of the soul than the shamans and witch doctors who preceded them. Nor, to tell the truth, have modern physicians who treat the ills of the flesh (if, indeed, it is possible to distinguish one from the other) fared much better.

Such inconclusive results after such large promises, however, also serve to exacerbate rather than mitigate our archaic negative response to doctors, though they do modify it somewhat, moving it from the pole of the horrific toward that of the comic. And the humor is compounded by our realization that finally the joke is on us, the patients; since in our time—as always—physicians and surgeons make a good living by failing to heal us. Small wonder, then, that the medical profession, in the Western world at least, has so often been treated (the euphemistic view of TV drama being an exception) satirically, ironically—though never, of course, without an undertone of horror. Indeed, one of the few inclusive overviews of images of physicians and surgeons during three millennia of our literature, concludes that they have been from beginning to end regarded as "arrogant, greedy and incompetent"—and treated therefore with tongue in cheek.

Cyrano de Bergerac (the historical, not the fictional one), for instance, observed wryly, "the fever assails us, the Physician kills us and the Priest sings"; while Montaigne wrote in a similar vein, "I notice no man is sooner sick or as late cured as the one who persists in a physician's care." In light of this, it seems scarcely surprising that the great popular playwrights from Shakespeare and Ben Jonson to Molière and George Bernard Shaw have long exploited this stereotypical view of the doctor for easy laughs. So, too, in the novel, Charles Dickens—though he has left us no single portrait of an M.D. as hilariously and wickedly memorable as his travesty of the "professional" nurse, Sairy Gamp—has created a whole gallery of satirical vignettes of doctors as (I quote now from a summary by one of his critics): "fools, drunkards, blackguards, criminals, ignorant men, impostors, solemn ignoramuses and clowns," plus, that critic adds rather ruefully, "a *few* gentlemen."

Moreover, ever since the Christianizing of the West, doctors have also been characterized as enemies of the true religion, deniers of the existence of God. By the late Middle Ages, the Latin tab "*Ubi tres medici, duo athei*" ("Where there are three doctors, there are two atheists") had already become proverbial. And mindful of this, perhaps, Chaucer observes of the "Doctor of Physic," who is one of his Canterbury Pilgrims, that not only does he love gold and split fees with his apothecaries, but also that "his study was little on the Bible."

It is a view of the profession that does not die out even with the emergence of the modern novel. In *Madame Bovary* (notable for its collection of incompetent and corrupt medical practitioners), Flaubert gives new life to what had become by then a rather weary stereotype, the quarrel between the village curé and the atheist medico—both in this case portrayed as buffoons and charlatans. And in his *Ulysses*, James Joyce characterizes Malachi Mulligan, leader of a pack of drunken medical students, as a particularly foulmouthed and obnoxious blasphemer, to whom the Virgin Birth is a dirty joke. Though in Joyce—as in Flaubert—the treatment of the Doctor as atheist remains comic in tone, the humor has become bitter indeed; and the next step is to the overt nausea and horror of Céline's *Journey to the End of the Night*—at which point the ill-kept secret is out.

Even as the sentimental fable of the Old Family Physician as Secular Savior from Marcus Welby to his descendants in *E.R.* represents a latter-day attempt to gloss over the dark side of our ambivalence, so the earlier jocular portrayal of the doctor as money-grubbing atheist represents another attempt at camouflage. But neither in the long run will hold; since what we unconsciously repress or consciously sublimate returns to haunt us in nightmares and the kind of mythic literature more faithful to those nightmares than our wish-fulfillment reveries.

Just such an archetypal legend very early on attached itself to the figure called Doctor Faustus: a self-declared enemy of the Christian God who, impatient with religious restrictions on research and experimentation, sells his soul to the Devil. To be sure, the Faust of medieval folktales or Christopher Marlowe's Renaissance tragedy or even Goethe's late-eighteenth-century dramatic poem was not an M.D. He is not even what we would call a "scientific" medical researcher, but rather a Master or, if you please, a Doctor of the then Forbidden Arts, which included alchemy and astrology as well as Black Magic. He has, however, become for the popular imagination a symbol of the hubris (and eventual damnation) of science, more particularly of experimental medicine; and we tend, therefore, to assimilate to his myth all advances in medical technology—from gene splicing to heart transplants and the chemical alteration of consciousness—that seem to threaten traditional values.

Not only has Faust provided the model for the stereotypical Mad Scientist of the comic books; but he has derived as a prototype for more complex figures, some of whom are, in the limited modern sense of the word, Doctors—and all of whom bear, like Faust himself, as a prefix inseparable from their names, the professional title we have come to associate with the image of a man in a long white coat bending over an operating table, a scalpel in his hand. Some of these malign doctors have appeared in stories which we consider high literature and therefore assign to our children in school: Nathaniel Hawthorne's Dr. Heidegger, for example, along with his Dr. Rappacinni and Dr. Grimshawe, who still seem, like Faust himself, more magicians than physicians—though, alas, they lack the archetypal resonance of the original on whom they are based.

That kind of resonance is to be found in legendary practitioners of what seems more like proper modern medicine, who appear in certain borderline "pop" books. I am thinking primarily of Dr. Frankenstein, Dr. Jekyll, and Dr. Moreau, though the list could be extended to include Dr. Caligari, Dr. Fu Manchu (who, improbably, was an M.D. from the University of Edinburgh), Dr. Strangelove, Dr. No, Dr. Hannibal Lecter, etc., etc. Like all genuine myths, these images of medical practitioners deliberately or inadvertently evil, trouble our sleep—before or after our periodic visits to the doctor, which of course we make all the same.

To be sure, we have all of us also been exposed to favorably portrayed physicians and surgeons, images which reinforce the more positive side of our ambivalence toward those who professionally invade our deepest privacies and share our most shameful fears. Such Good Doctors appear not only in popular TV dramas, they are also present in literature which we prize more highly, ranging from Lydgate in George Eliot's *Middlemarch* to Martin Arrowsmith in Sinclair Lewis's eponymous novel. Even certain "good" real-life physicians and medical researchers, like Dr. Pasteur, Dr. Salk, Dr. Spock, and (for some) Dr. Freud, have been, as it were, mythologized as sages and saviors by the press.

Yet, alas, none of these more benign figures possesses our imaginations deeply enough to have achieved the mythological status of, say, the malign Dr. Mengele: the infamous experimenter on dwarfs and twins, for whom Hitler's Death Camps provided an ideal laboratory; and whose image is, therefore, easily assimilable to that foreshadowed in Dr. Faustus and fully realized in Drs. Frankenstein, Jekyll, and Moreau. It is, in any case, with these three characters that we must come to terms, if we would understand how the Faustian archetype was altered in response to the development of modern medical technology: the Black Magician transmogrified into the Man in the White Coat, in what eventually comes to be known as Science Fiction.

For a while, indeed, other mythic themes threatened to replace that ancient archetype in the new genre. These included Time Travel, Robotics, faster-than-the-speed-of-light Space Flight, and especially the End of Man. Moreover, since the typically utopian pop writers of the "Golden Age" of science fiction considered all technology as ultimately salvational, it was left to dystopian mainstream interlopers into that genre, like Evgeny Zamyatin, Aldous Huxley, and Anthony Burgess to create images of a future dominated by evil doctors. In Zamyatin's *We*, for instance, freedom-loving dissidents are sent to the "Operations Department" for therapeutic lobotomies; while in Huxley's *Brave New World* conformity is insured by selective breeding, cloning (which he calls "Bokhanization"), extra-uterine conception, neo-Pavlovian conditioning, and the administration of tranquilizing drugs.

Finally, faith in science had replaced the traditional belief in God. "God is concompatible with machinery and scientific medicine and happiness," an apologist for his New Order declares. And in Burgess' *A Clockwork Orange*, a future is envisaged in which the medical profession had sought by techniques of behavior modification to eliminate all possibilities of antisocial violence had ended by destroying free will.

Yet all this changed again when the original tiny audience for sci-fi was swelled by a host of new readers, and a new generation of writers appeared, the so-called "New Wave," who addressed that audience—responding like them to the Cultural Revolution of the sixties. The dissident young of those troubled times, when they read for pleasure, turned not to the Great Books urged on them by their English teachers but to the sort of fantasy and science fiction that their teachers despised. So, too, when they went to the movies it was not to see the European "art films" admired by critics but the horror flicks made in America some thirty years before—most notably, of course *Dracula, Frankenstein*, and *Dr. Jekyll and Mr. Hyde*. Not completely satisfied with the older versions, moreover, they demanded bloodier and more erotic new versions, able both to feed their free-floating paranoia and reinforce their iatrophobia.

Though such iatrophobia has always been with us, it assumed an especially virulent form in the sixties. This was due, no doubt, to the growing awareness of the insidious role played by medicos during Hitler's regime: not just the infamous experiments of Dr. Mengele, but the less notorious efforts of Dr. Étienne Wolff of Strassbourg, who (with the Führer's blessing) produced monster births in animals and was, apparently, already planning to do so with humans when the Third Reich fell. But surely the revelation in the American press of the birth of the Thalidomide babies had some effect, too. The post-World War II world had dreamed of the appearance of monstrous mutants as a result of the dropping of the Bomb; but when a considerable number of congenital malformations did appear, they were not the result of atomic radiation but of ill-advised medication administered by physicians to prevent nausea in early pregnancy: iatrogenic freaks, in short.

Moreover, doctors had become politically suspect as well, since in that time of Right/Left polarization, they were by and large on the Right. Certainly, the AMA was a staunch defender of what was called in the jargon of the times "the military-industrial complex." And, as I myself am old enough to remember, in the heyday of the Counter Culture on campus, it was the medical faculties which took the hardest line against not merely the violent excesses of the student revolutionaries but their agitation on behalf of Civil Rights and against the Vietnam War. Small wonder, then, that in some quarters even now, Doctors (still predominantly White and male, though somewhat more liberal perhaps) continue to be regarded as defenders of a dying status quo: racist and sexist almost by definition. It is indeed one of the basic dogmas of Radical Feminism that physicians and surgeons are the enemies of women, contemptuous of their bodies and prone to label their complaints pathological.

In any case, whatever their avowed or implicit politics, practitioners of medicine with diplomas and degrees were distrusted in a time when, for an articulate minority, "professional" had become a dirty word, and do-it-yourself an honorific one. They considered it virtuous not only to do home carpentry and change one's own spark plugs but also to "birth" one's own babies and to treat cancer with self-prescribed home remedies, ranging from Orgone Boxes, acupuncture, and microbiotic diets to herbal medications from the Old Wives' Pharmacopeia.

TYRANNY OF THE NORMAL

Nor has the influence of such notions ceased even at the century's end, when the Counter Culture has—without having achieved any of its major political goals—become part of the Over-the-Counter Culture. Only a very few hardcore iatrophobes any longer advise eschewing routine medical procedures like inoculation and vaccination. Our daily newspapers, however, continue to print daily columns by so-called "People's Doctors" warning us away from the medication family physicians are most likely to prescribe in favor of herbal cures, "holistic medicine," and diets free from salt, sugar, fat, and red meat.

Even those of us who pay as little attention to such columns as to the daily horoscope, tend these days to approach doctors less as trusting patients than as wary consumers—resolved in advance to sue if anything goes wrong. Moreover, scarcely any of us who lived through the anti-institutional brainwashing of the sixties can enter a hospital without fear and trembling. We may be aware at this point that without the centralization and bureaucratic organization of medical care, certain diagnostic and therapeutic breakthroughs would never have occurred. Yet we cannot quite forget the other half of the truth about hospitals that the spokesman of the sixties forced us to confront: that they tend to be soulless and inhumane, as rigidly hierarchal and totalitarian as a prison or army barracks. And that they are in some sense, therefore—whatever the good intentions of their staffs—anti-therapeutic: not just accidental breeding grounds of disease, but places that teach patients to be sick rather than to get well; if, indeed (as the more radical critics suggested), what health professionals call "getting well" is a goal to be desired at all.

It was especially the concept of "mental health" as professionally defined that was called into question in the era of dissent. Consequently, the doctors and nurses who tried to enforce it by psychochemistry, shock treatment, and lobotomy were regarded with especial distrust: as a kind of white-jacketed thought police in service of the oppressive state, to be resisted, if and when the necessity arose, with the same guerilla tactics as bluecoated cops attempting to break up a campus demonstration. I can, for example, remember attending in the early seventies a "Conference on Madness" organized by students and faculty of a major university, at which—after a long, passionate defense by a disciple of R. D. Laing of schizophrenia as a breakthrough into hitherto unexplored areas of consciousness—most of the audience marched off to destroy the shock-therapy apparatus at a nearby hospital.

At that point, I must confess, I fled, so that I never knew whether or not they finally succeeded in smashing those machines. What I do know is that they did succeed in persuading a large number of others, both old and young, that all shrinks, indeed, all doctors are the enemies of freedom. Certainly that became a central theme in the work of "New Wave" writers like John Brunner, Philip K. Dick, Brian Aldiss, and J. G. Ballard, who, coming of age in the sixties, were not merely observers of but participants in the dissenting political and deviant lifestyles of the Counter Culture. In any case, they carried the early dystopians' attack on modern medical procedures to its ultimate conclusion. That is to say, they rejected lock, stock, and barrel the euphoric vision of a world free of disease, neurosis, and eventually death itself, in whose name those procedures were justified.

On the face of it, it must be confessed, that vision seemed plausible enough. After all, certain diseases which had plagued mankind for millennia (leprosy, for instance, and small pox and polio) seemed at the point of disappearing. Besides which, it had become possible for more and more of us to survive traumatic heart attacks and even some forms of cancer for lengthier periods of time. And even as our life expectancy increased, we were, it seemed, moving ever closer to being able to stay young and beautiful as long as our lives could be made to last: already techniques were available for concealing the ravages of time once thought irreversible.

So, too, thanks to medical research and experiment, did dismayed parents no longer have to accept as inevitable the birth of those "congenital malformations" that once undercut our faith in the continuous upward and onward evolution of our species. Even now such "freaks of nature" can be detected early enough for preventive abortions; and even after birth, they can be, in some cases at least, "repaired." Moreover, medical researchers are learning at this very moment to read our DNA codes so that genetic manipulation before conception seems just around the corner.

Such breakthroughs, however, have been regarded by the new dystopians not with elation but horror. John Brunner, for instance, already in 1968 in his *Stand on Zanzibar* warned his readers against the perils of "compulsory artificial optimization of the embryo." Then a dozen years later in *Players at the Game of People*, having realized that such "optimization" might well turn out to be available only to a privileged few, he speculated on the price those chosen might be required to pay for the prolongation of life and the preservation of physical beauty. That the price for such ersatz immortality turns out to be their souls is scarcely a surprise; since the bargain they strike—though this time not with the Devil but with aliens from Outer Space—is the latest version of the Faustian Pact.

Why then, for all its virtues does Brunner's retelling of that archetypal tale lack the mythic resonance of Goethe's original telling and the three earlier classic retellings by Mary Shelley, R. L. Stevenson, and H. G. Wells? It is not, surely, because science fiction and fantasy have in the second half of this century lost their original mythopoeic power. After all, archetypal characters from other contemporary works in that genre—notably Robert Heinlein's Valentine Michael Smith, Isaac Asimov's Robie the Robot, as well as Captain Kirk and Mr. Spock from the multiauthored *Star Trek*—live on in our collective consciousness the life of true myths.

It is rather, perhaps, because Drs. Frankenstein, Jekyll, and Moreau still preempt our imaginations so deeply that they need not, indeed, cannot, be replaced. Aware of this, some recent sci-fi authors have instead settled for trying to kidnap them, to make them their own, as it were, at second hand. So, for instance, Brian Aldiss (not merely a talented practitioner of the genre, but one of its best critics) has attempted in *Frankenstein Unbound* (1973) and *An Island of Dr. Moreau* (1987).

Meanwhile in the post-print media these Doctors and their Monsters, especially Frankenstein and his, have recently undergone a strange—and to me somewhat surprising—change; having been transformed by parody and burlesque into occasions for laughter rather than terror. It is not, let me be clear, that Frankenstein travesties like Mel Brooks's *Young Frankenstein* or the filmed British musical *The Rocky Horror Picture Show* (both made in the mid-seventies) turn the Bad Doctor back from the figure of horror he became after Mary Shelley to the figure of fun that he was to many in the Middle Ages and the Renaissance. Rather, such travesties seek to persuade us that Frankenstein is, and has always been, laughable precisely *because* he is truly horrific; or, at least, that we must, if we are to preserve our sanity in a world where hubristic medical science plays an ever larger and more sinister role, manage to laugh at the doctor without denying or euphemizing the horror he represents.

It is easy—a little too easy, perhaps—to dismiss *Young Frankenstein* as mere slapstick, an obvious parody of an archetype turned cliché. And it may well be that for this reason it has never achieved the cult status of *The Rocky Horror Picture Show*. The latter is not only more blatantly parodic (the Doctor is called Frankenfurter) and more grossly erotic (both he and his monster, Rocky, are revealed as transvestitites and transsexuals), but also more disgustingly horrific (the doctor turns out to be a murderer who serves up his victim in a cannibalistic feast). Finally *The Rocky Horror Picture Show* breaks almost all the taboos in which our liberated and permissive society still vestigially believes, becoming in the process a kind of Black Mass pretending it is a shaggy dog joke.

In this version, at any rate, the tale of Frankenstein has ceased to be literature or even entertainment and has become a kind of secular ritual. Played in neighborhood theaters throughout the world at the mythic hour of midnight on Fridays and Saturdays, it is attended (not once or twice, but over and over) by communicants, ceremonially garbed and prepared not to watch but to respond like participants in a religious ceremony or a witches' sabbath. There is not now, nor has there ever been, I think, a pop version of an archetypal tale that has moved its audience in quite this way. And for our purposes it is instructive to realize that at the heart of its symbolic action is an ambiguous monster flanked by its even more ambiguous and monstrous creator: the doctor with many names but only a single face—the face of evil with good intentions.

Images of the Nurse
in Fiction and Popular Culture

>∈

ALL SUBCOMMUNITIES (ethnic, generational, sexual, professional) that constitute the total community of humankind are perceived by others through myths or stereotypes that more often
than not they find offensive—not merely slanderous but objectively "untrue," i.e., unlike certain more favorable images through
which they would prefer to be perceived. I was reminded of this
the other day when I read in the letter columns of my local newspaper a heartfelt protest from a Registered Nurse that began,
"When the ward nurse comes up in conversation, what do you
think of? Do images of Mary Benjamin, Hot Lips Houlihan and
Nurse Ripples come to mind? Or do you think of the harried young
woman with blood spattered on her uniform who answered the
call like the last time you or your loved one was hospitalized?"
Quite clearly, the mind of the protestor herself is, like the minds
of all the rest of us, possessed by the stereotypes she resents. And
how could it be otherwise, since we are all bombarded day and
night, so unremittingly that after a while we are scarcely aware of
it, by movie and TV versions of the Nurse which are themselves as
much "facts" of our experience as actual Nurses themselves.
Indeed, there is scarcely anything on the tube these days in which
such images do not appear. I am thinking not only of doctor shows
from *Dr. Kildare* to *E.R.*, but also of the continuing success of the
series *M*A*S*H*, which made "Hot Lips" perhaps the best known
Nurse figure of all time; not to mention the so-called "soaps,"
which preempt the daylight hours on television.

In the latter, nurses are omnipresent since their typical setting is an enclosed space, and the feelings in which they specialize are pain, suffering, and bereavement. What more appropriate then to the form than the sickroom or the hospital?

Moreover, since the audience for such shows is largely—though not, of course, exclusively—women, many of their main characters are women, some of them inevitably Nurses; since an archetypal, *the* archetypal female profession has long been nursing—as the names by which its practitioners are called clearly reveal. "Nurse," after all, signifies "nurturer," "milk-giver"; which is to say, Mother or surrogate mother. And the alternative title used by the English, "Sister," complicates the matter even further with associations ecclesiastical or familial, but always female.

In the popular mind, the deep psyche of the mass audience, not merely (in contempt of the changing facts of the case) does Nurse equal Woman, but, on an even profounder mythological level, Woman equals Nurse. This means that many ancient (male) stereotypes of females in general are transferred automatically to the specific category of nurses. The latter are, in any case, portrayed as being still what many women refuse to be: subordinate to men, faithful, passive executors of their orders. They are, therefore, in their role of sustainers and supporters, presented sympathetically—as, say, women business executives, who also appear on the Soaps, are typically not.

But it is not quite as simple as this. After all, nurses preside at the bedsides of males—privileged, even required, unlike other members of their sex—except for prostitutes—to touch, handle, manipulate the naked flesh of males. And they tend, therefore, to be portrayed also as erotic figures of a peculiar, ambiguous kind. In other words, they are presented as being at once theoretically taboo (this their uniforms declare, white, cool, starched, reminiscent of the habits of Nuns pledged to eternal chastity); and, or at least so the lubricious dreams of the opposite sex have always insisted, not merely sexually desirable, but available, ready, and willing. Certainly, the line about nurses as potential dates in the

movie version of *Marty*, "money in the bank," evokes the stereotype of their being always at the point of tumbling into the sack,
whether to win the heart of a well-heeled patient, or to achieve
upward social mobility by marrying a doctor, or simply out of
sheer, uninhibited lust. In any case, in the popular arts, nurses are
typically portrayed as pursued by or pursuing patients, making
passes at or being approached by interns or residents.

But even this is not quite the whole story; since nurses, once
they are promoted from neophytes to Head Nurses, are no longer
imagined as sexually vulnerable sisters but rather as equivocal,
asexual mothers. Sometimes they are conceived as Good Mamas,
but more often as Bad ones: bullying, blustering, or condescending to the full-grown men helpless in their hands ("It's time for us
to take our medication. Why don't you sit up tall like a good boy?")
as if they were dependent children. All of us (women as well as
men) lived once as infants and toddlers under a total matriarchy;
and men especially have nightmares of regressing to that state of
total dependence, nightmares likely to recur in a hospital bed and
inevitably projected upon the attendant nurse.

Obviously, all of these stereotypes of the nurse, endlessly reit-
erated on the screen large or small, existed long before movies or
television. Indeed, the archetypes that underlie them are older
even than the profession of nursing, as old as patriarchal society
itself. But they were profoundly modified by the emergence of that
profession some hundred and fifty years ago, when they were fixed
in certain "classic" books that we still read, and in more recent
ones that still transmit stereotypes created in the Age of Victoria.
Less ephemeral and more respectable than TV shows or B-movies,
such books are preserved in libraries and assigned in classrooms—
giving them a special kind of authority. From this point in, therefore, I shall refer chiefly to them; concentrating, indeed, on those
that I have myself required of my own students or written about in
critical studies.

First, however, I feel obliged to mention in passing certain works of nonfiction, which have mythologized the lives and achievement of actual nurses. Some of these accounts were written as public-relations releases for the still struggling profession, some as propaganda for political causes associated with that profession because of its connection with the military establishments of various modern nation states. It was such literature that helped to create favorable images of nurses in the course of turning two major figures, Florence Nightingale and Edith Cavell, first into celebrities and then into legends.

Both were combat nurses, tending wounded troops as only male orderlies had in earlier times—and both were, of course, British. Yet both became known worldwide almost immediately. Cavell, to be sure, was a participant in the first war general enough to be called a World War; but Nightingale took part in a limited parochial engagement, the ill-fated English attempt to invade the Crimea. Yet a couple of generations of girls were called "Florence" after Nightingale, and a mountain in Western New York still bears the name of Cavell. It was perhaps the rising tide of feminism (though Nightingale was strongly anti-feminist, declaring herself "brutally indifferent" to the plight of women qua women), or simply the need for female heroes in a time when only men were actual warriors, that explains their appeal.

Certainly it was not the literary quality of the documents which attempted to glorify them; since these are by and large shameless schlock produced by nameless hacks, whose appeal was based on values that have since become suspect to anyone with the slightest degree of sophistication. Most of us—several wars later and in a time of revulsion from jingoism of all sorts—are more likely to be embarrassed than moved by the illustrated tracts showing Edith Cavell going down before the bullets of a German firing squad: a martyr to the brutality of the Dirty Huns, whom our forefathers and mothers loved to hate. Actually, Cavell was executed after a reasonably fair war crimes trial at the hands of the German Army, accused (on the basis of convincing evidence) of collaboration with the Belgian Underground and British Intelligence, while using her nurse's role as cover. Her last words, moreover, were reportedly "Patriotism is not enough": a disconcerting remark which was kept an official secret until the time of maximum pacifism between two Great Wars. Small wonder, then, that the literature which created it has disappeared, though the myth of Cavell as Martyr Nurse somehow survives.

We continue to reprint, however, in more scholarly later biographies, the earliest sentimental-patriotic-heroic accounts of Florence Nightingale's mission to the troops of the Crimea, which established in the mind of the world the image of the Nurse as "The Lady with a Lamp," a source of Light in the gathering Darkness. Yet we tend to read them with the same amused condescension as we do the verses she inspired from the Pop poets of her time (admirably sincere but hopelessly inept):

> She prays for the dying, she gives peace to the brave,
> She feels that the soldier has a soul to be saved,
> The wounded they love her as it has been seen.
> She's the soldier's preserver, they call her the Queen.
> May God give her strength, and her heart never fail,
> One of Heaven's best gifts is Miss Nightingale.

It is ironical enough that her image as the nurse par excellence has survived nationalism, imperialism, and simpleminded missionary zeal, as well as the taste for such poetry. But even more ironical is the fact that similar favorable images of the profession are preserved only in the subliterature which celebrates those values; these days in novels intended for subteens of all ages, books with titles like *Doctor Gregory's Debutante Nurse*, *Nurse Ann's Dream Doctor*, *Theatre Sister in Love*, *Mink on My Apron*, and of course, *Hold the Lamp High* and *Reluctant Nightingale*. More serious books, however, which is to say books taken seriously by critics and schoolteachers, are likely still to deal with nurses, as they always have, at worst negatively, at best equivocally.

One of the most wicked of all such wicked caricatures of nurses is the very first—or in any case the earliest still in print and listed under the subcategory of "nurses" in classified bibliographies of fiction. I am referring, of course, to Sairey Gamp, who made her appearance in Charles Dickens's *Martin Chuzzlewit*, initially published in book form in 1844: the very year in which Florence Nightingale finally decided—hearing mysterious voices from heaven—to dedicate herself to a career of nursing. *Martin Chuzzlewit* is not currently one of the favorite novels of Dickens, having been replaced in critical favor by *David Copperfield*, *Great Expectations*, even *Hard Times*. But I have always admired it for its malicious portrayal of mid-nineteenth-century America, its oleaginous villain, Pecksniff, and especially for that large, slovenly, voracious, drunken, endlessly garrulous guardian of the childbed, the sickroom, and the mortuary, Mrs. Gamp. Along with an imaginary companion and interlocutor, she is introduced as a minor character but threatens finally to take over the whole of the book, though she remains peripheral to its main plot.

What she reflects clearly is Dickens's attitude toward nurses, both amateur, which she is in fact, and "professional," which she outrageously claims to be, though she is the very antitype of everything Florence Nightingale dreamed that profession might become. When she is not shamelessly neglecting her patients, she is sadistically punching them, strangling them—presumably in an attempt to induce them to ingest medication—or pushing them closer and closer to the open fire in an effort to "soothe their minds" by a kind of shock treatment that verges on burning them alive. Meanwhile, she is cadging food, drink, and hand-me-down clothes and, of course, talking, talking, talking...

Scandalous as this portrait may be, it can scarcely be denied that it is in some ways "true to life," i.e., a fair representation of what many, perhaps most, nurses were before the reforms of Nightingale and other Christian Ladies bent on redeeming nursing from its original plebeian practitioners. As a matter of fact, Dickens had actually cleaned up Sairey a little, presumably to avoid shocking his genteel audience; portraying her, that is to say, as a celibate though alcoholic widow rather than a prostitute and/or bawd, as indeed many such early Victorian nurses were.

What intrigues us still about Sairey Gamp, however, is the mythic nightmare figure which persists just beneath her "realistic," satiric surfaces, and the archaic fears of Woman as Witch that figure embodies. Typically unconscious in writer and reader alike, those fears provide a clue to the hostility toward nurses which popular literature strives to conceal by sentimentalizing and idealization, and books like Dickens's try to exorcise with ridicule. It pays to notice in this light just what it is that Mrs. Gamp *does*. Not only does she provide care for the sick, day and night; but she also delivers babies and prepares corpses for burial. Lying-in and laying-out are still her province, as they were the province of women exclusively before the patriarchal revolution that turned them over to "professional" male obstetricians and funeral directors. Only the tending of the ill (perhaps because it is the least terrifying and taboo of the original threefold functions) was left to women.

Sairey Gamp, however, still practices all three of the traditional mysteries of life and death originally associated, along with the expurgated final mystery of Sex, with the Great Mother, the White Goddess; and which, after the emergence of patriarchal deities, survived in the underground religion as the province of the "Wise Women" or Witches. It is in any case as a Witch, albeit a comic one, that Sairey Gamp is portrayed: one in whose unclean hands all three traditional functions turn malignant. Not only does her actual practice travesty the role of bedside healer to which she lays claim, but even more as midwife and layer-out of the dead her skills are shown as debouching in mutilation and monstrosity. Early on in the novel, we hear her talking of her first corpse, her own husband, whom she describes as stretched out stark and cold "with a penny piece on each eye, and his wooden leg under his left arm."

And toward the end, she recounts having come on her imaginary friend's "sweet infant...kep' in spirits in a bottle..." and therefore displayed in a traveling show of freaks "in company with the pink-eyed lady, Prooshan dwarf, and livin' skelinton..."

But Dickens wants to have it both ways: evoking contempt from his readers for the persistence in Mrs. Gamp of what is still archaic (still resistant to the rationalization and hierarchization of the medical profession), but also for her claims to absolute authority in the sickroom in the name of professionalism. In chapter headings and in the text, Dickens uses the word "professional" over and over as a term of contempt making it clear that he objects not only to the shamanistic past of nursing but to the scientific, bureaucratic future imagined for it by Florence Nightingale. Not that he is opposed to demystification; what he advocates is humanization rather than professionalization or certification. This he makes clear in the parting words of advice given by old Martin Chuzzlewit to a discomfited Mrs. Gamp: "...a little less liquor, and a little more humanity, and a little less regard for herself, and a little more regard for her patients, and perhaps a trifle of additional honesty."

In any case, Dickens's two-pronged indictment of nurses suggests a double bind, a no-win situation for the profession, out of which—at least in the imagination of the makers of our most respected books—they still struggle in vain to extricate themselves. Certainly, this is true of Ken Kesey's *One Flew Over the Cuckoo's Nest*, published in 1962, more than a century after *Martin Chuzzlewit*. Before discussing it, however, there are certain works that appeared in the years between, which demand to be mentioned in passing though none of them possesses equal archetypal resonance.

The first is an extraordinary poem by the greatest of American poets, the only major writer to deal with nurses who had actually been a nurse—combat nurse, in fact, quite like Florence Nightingale and Edith Cavell. This was, of course, Walt Whitman, who just after the end of the American Civil War (once more in the reign of Queen Victoria) added to his continually revised epic, *Leaves of Grass*, a section called "Drum-Taps," at the very center of which stands "The Wound-Dresser." From the beginning of his career as a poet, Whitman had been possessed by an image of himself as a comforter of the Afflicted, a healing presence at the bedside of the Sick. In "The Sleepers," one of the twelve poems published in the first edition of *Leaves of Grass*, he wrote, for instance, "I stand in the dark with drooping eyes by the worstsuffering and the most restless / I pass my hands soothingly to and fro a few inches from them, / The restless sink in their beds, they fitfully sleep" (lines 23-25).

During the Civil War, however, Whitman actually tended the wounded in military hospitals in Washington, DC, turning fantasy into fact and fact back into poetry:

> Bearing the bandages, water and sponge,
> Straight and swift to my wounded I go,
> Where they lie on the ground after the battle brought in,
> Where their priceless blood reddens the grass, the
>   ground,
> . . . .
> From the stump of the arm, the amputated hand,
> I undo the clotted lint, remove the slough, wash off the
>   matter and blood,
> Back on his pillow the soldier bends with curv'd neck
>   and side-falling head,
> His eyes are closed, his face is pale, he dares not look on
>   the bloody stump,
> And has not yet look'd on it.
> . . . .
> I dress the perforated shoulder, the foot with the bullet-
>   wound,
> Cleanse the one with a gnawing and putrid gangrene, so
>   sickening, so offensive,
> While the attendant stands behind aside me holding the
>   tray and pail.

I am faithful, I do not give out,
The fractur'd thigh, the knee, the wound in the
    abdomen,
These and more I dress with impassive hand, (yet deep in
    my breast a fire, a burning flame.)

Thus in silence in dreams' projections,
Returning, resuming, I thread my way through the
    hospitals,
The hurt and wounded I pacify with soothing hand,
I sit by the restless all the dark night, some are so young,
Some suffer so much, I recall the experience sweet and sad,
(Many a soldier's loving arms about this neck have
    cross'd and rested,
Many a soldier's kiss dwells on these bearded lips.)

Most people, however, remembering images of nurses in literature do not recall this poem, in part because Whitman was of the wrong gender, a male pretender to a role which mythologically we associate with the female of the species. Moreover, his vision of the *eros* of nursing, the sexual overtones of the bedside encounter with the maimed and the wounded, is disturbingly ambiguous, containing hints of lubricity and sado-masochism compatible neither with the benign popular cliché of the nurse as a sexless secular saint, nor the Gamp anti-stereotype of an equally sexless though malevolent exploiter of her patients. Especially disconcerting to the readers of Whitman's own time—and to many still, even in our "enlightened" age—are the homosexual implications of his verses. Nonetheless, "The Wound-Dresser" remains the most moving and subtle evocation in print of the experience of nursing in a time of war—*from the viewpoint of the nurse.*
    When, however, some fifty years later, in Ernest Hemingway's *A Farewell to Arms*, another American writer, out of his own experience in another major war, attempted to evoke (this time in prose) the figure of the nurse, it was from the viewpoint of the

nursed. Unlike Whitman, Hemingway, though he was not a combatant (he served as a volunteer with the Italian Ambulance Corps), was also not a nurse. Moreover, he reimagines his semi-autobiographical protagonist, Lieutenant Henry, as a soldier who, after being drastically wounded, manages to survive World War I to tell his tale. It is his nurse, Catherine Barkley, who dies—as seems at first improbable but finally appropriate enough in a time haunted by the legend of Edith Cavell, who was killed in the midst of combat. Still, Catherine does not like the latter die at the hands of a German firing squad but in childbirth; condemned by her author, for reasons best known to himself, to meet her end in the hospital where she has gone hoping to produce new life.

Finally, the figure of Catherine Barkley, however pathetic, remains too conventional, too like the Pop stereotype of the nurse to remain in our conscious minds, much less to haunt our dreams. Passive, obedient, utterly subject to the wills of her medical superiors and her lover, wanting desperately to be "a good girl" but unable to deny the wounded soldier her bed, she provides an erotic alternative to the thanatic desolation of war. But somehow we never quite believe in her. Indeed, there is a kind of critical consensus that there is only one real rounded character in Hemingway's novel, Henry himself; the rest, including Catherine, are ghosts even before they die.

Moreover, just as in *A Farewell to Arms* Catherine produced no viable offspring, so too as literary prototype she inspired no notable protagonists in the best-loved fiction of the thirties, forties, and fifties. Not, in fact, until the late sixties, the period of the Counter Culture, did the nurse reemerge as a central figure; this time in the cult literature of the young—particularly in two underground favorites, Robert Heinlein's *Stranger in a Strange Land* and, as mentioned before, Kesey's *One Flew Over the Cuckoo's Nest.*

It is, however, almost impossible to remember that the major female character in *Stranger in a Strange Land* is a nurse, despite the fact that Heinlein announces in the opening pages that

"Gillian Boardman was a competent nurse and her hobby was men." When the male protagonist, who has been brought up on Mars, arrives on earth weak and helpless as a baby, she bustles about his hospital bed, speaking in the regal first person plural as we have learned from TV shows all nurses do, "'Well, how are we today? Feeling better?'" Before the book's end, however, even the author seems to have forgotten her profession, letting her blend into the scarcely individualized gaggle of good lays—the secretaries, sideshow entertainers, and strippers—who constitute the whole of his female cast. Indeed, eventually Gillian becomes a stripper, too, and at last an avatar of the Earth Goddess, the incarnation of female sexuality in the half-fraudulent ritual of a communal cult, in which all the men possess all the women turn and turn about. She represents, that is to say, little more than the ancient cliché of the nurse as erotic object raised to its highest power; and she tends to fade therefore from the memories of those who read the book in quest of something up-to-date: an advocacy of cannibalism, let's say, or of sex without commitment or guilt.

Heinlein's was the first work of avowed science fiction to become a best-seller, and it continues to be reprinted more than thirty years later. But though it added the new verb, to grok, to the language and in the middle sixties provided rituals for Charles Manson's murderous "religion," none of its women characters are of truly mythic dimensions—certainly not its single nurse. Such an authentically archetypal character did appear, however, in an even more brutally misogynous novel published at about the same time, *One Flew Over the Cuckoo's Nest*, which takes place in the psychiatric ward of the State Hospital, presided over by a monster in female form known as Nurse Ratched, or more familiarly, "Big Nurse." That larger-than-life tyrant of the ward does not quite attain the full archetypal dimensions of other memorable women in our literature, Hester Prynne, for instance (who ends up playing a nursely role in the community that casts her out), or even Scarlett O'Hara (who fails miserably in her attempt to become a

Civil War wound-dresser à la Walt Whitman). Yet Ratched has become a byword and a myth over the twenty years since her first appearance—replacing Sairey Gamp for the contemporary reader as the mythic nurse par excellence.

But how different she is from her predecessor: not slovenly but neat to a fault—encased in ironed and starched white garb, spotless, unspottable. Moreover, far from being a drunk, she is the enemy of booze, even as she is the enemy of sexual promiscuity, gambling, all hedonism and moral laxness. A super-professional rather than a helpless amateur, she is organized and the organizer of everyone around her: just such an efficient administrator, in fact, as Florence Nightingale dreamed and became. Though she is not portrayed as a combat nurse, we are told that Ratched has learned her trade, grown old and rigid while serving in the Army—finally introjecting the values of the modern military into the routine of the hospital, as Nightingale also dreamed that nurses of the future might do.

But Big Nurse remains for Kesey even more hateful; since she is no longer comic and cannot be laughed away, any more than she can be brought into line (as Mrs. Gamp could still be) by a threat to call the police. She has become the police; and can therefore only be subdued through an act of outlawry, like the rapist's murderous assault, vain but gallant, made on her by the book's major male character, R. P. McMurphy. In part Kesey's attitude can be explained by the age which bred him and whose spokesman he became: a revolutionary time, when all hierarchal institutions, not least the hospital, had come to be despised, and all professions, specialties—especially, perhaps, medical ones, and most especially psychiatry—were regarded with hostility and suspicion.

But disconcertingly, Big Nurse is also hated and feared for what she has in common with Mrs. Gamp: i.e., for being a woman; and the equation of woman and nurse persists in the deep male psyche despite superficial changes in the profession. For McMurphy, her attempt to "cure" psychosis—i.e, force all psychological deviants into conformity with the system—seems a kind of ball-breaking: a war against manhood, which beginning with the administration of tranquilizers moves on to electroshock therapy, then reveals its true motive when it climaxes in lobotomy—the ultimate form of castration. To Kesey, indeed, all women—except possibly prostitutes—represent Bad Mama, which is to say, mother after she has withdrawn the breast (and Nurse Ratched is portrayed as the biggest-titted white mother of them all under her starched uniform) and taken up the rod. Freedom, therefore, is to be found only in a constant flight from them and all they represent. Otherwise the American male is doomed to end up a cog in the machine, like most of the great world outside the asylum: a self-castrated victim like Billy Bibbit, or a mere vegetable like McMurphy after his failed attempt to reach the living flesh beneath Ratched's pristine whites.

Such attitudes are based on a special American brand of machismo and misogyny much older than the Cultural Revolution—as old, indeed, as our literature itself, beginning with the revolt of Rip Van Winkle against what Washington Irving called "petticoat tyranny." In this view, women—especially White women, imbued with the values of European Christianity—represent not what Sairey Gamp still symbolized for Dickens: the anarchy of the unconscious, the primordial and the archaic; but rather consciousness, conscience, repression: what Huck Finn, about to flee into the Wilderness, calls "Sivilization." It seems inevitable in light of this that when nurses have ceased to be thought of as vestigial witches and are reimagined as machine tenders, soulless machines themselves, it should be an American author who bestows on them their new mythological name.

What is baffling is that the American public, male and female, continues to hate Nurse Ratched and to love McMurphy for his failed assault on her, not merely as they live on in the still-reprinted novel but as they were reborn in the late seventies in an immensely successful movie. What our response betrays is the persistence of attitudes we like to think we have long outgrown, not just toward nurses but toward all women whom that profession still mythologically represents. And perhaps, after all, it is the function of literature to remind us (though for better or for worse, who can say?) of precisely such otherwise unconfessed impulses: the dark side of our ambivalence toward both those who bear us and those who tend us when we are ill.

Why Organ Transplant Programs Do Not Succeed

⇥⇤

FROM THE START, there have been two major obstacles to the success of organ transplant programs, both of which can be called by the single name "rejection." Most often that term is applied metaphorically to a host body's stubborn refusal to accept the organs of another as its own; and since such reactions are purely somatic, physiological, chemical, their solutions are sought and sometimes successfully found in the laboratory. In ordinary usage, however, "rejection" implies volition, a psychological response not soluble by mechanical means. Less metaphorically, then, it can be used to describe the failure of the majority of our population to become organ donors, which has caused the ever-growing gap between supply and demand that so vexes the sponsors of transplant programs. Especially vexing to them is the reluctance of young males (the optimum field for organ harvesting) to pledge parts of their bodies for posthumous donation—or of surviving family members to permit their dismemberment after death.

To deal with this sort of "rejection" involves making changes not in the soma but in the psyche. This would be difficult enough in any case, but what makes it especially so is that the attitudes which underlie it are rooted in fears and fantasies below the level of full consciousness. Clear evidence of this is to be found in the fact that when asked by pollsters, 90 percent of the same population that actually resists organ transplantation indicates a willingness, even an eagerness to do so. There is, that is to say, a puzzling contradiction between what most potential donors say they are prepared to do and what most of them end up doing.

This is not mere hypocrisy. Rather it is the result of a profound, though quite unsuspected, contradiction between the conscious acceptance and the unconscious repulsion which many of us— perhaps, to some degree, all of us—feel when confronted with a presumably benign surgical procedure that challenges our most deep-seated, primal notions about life and death, the self and the other, body and spirit: a procedure, moreover, conducted without any of the consoling rituals traditionally accorded the cadavers of our beloved ones.

In light of this, it is evident that the naive strategies of indoctrination currently used to persuade the young to become donors of their own body parts will not work. Certainly not the one I recently received through the mails, urging that required courses on the benefits of organ donation be given in all high schools, along with those in safe driving. It is a persuasive technique equaled in its naivete only by the Donor Award Patches currently being offered by the Boy Scouts of America to members who pledge to "give the gift of life." Both use pious and humane metaphors that are presumably more effective in moving the general public than the horticultural ones employed by medical professionals talking to each other—like "transplantation" and "harvesting."

Yet though less dehumanizing, even these religious figures of speech are likely to be greeted with skepticism by the street-wise disenchanted young men (many of them underclass and/or black), who are the suicides or victims of traffic accidents and urban violence that provide the most suitable *membra disjecta* for transplantation. Indeed, they are unlikely to persuade very many of any gender, race, or class at the deep psychic levels where instinctive rejection occurs. It is, therefore, to these deep levels and their underlying myths that we must look if we are to come to terms with the problem of psychological rejection. I say "come to terms" rather than "overcome" because I am not sure that we can overcome it in the foreseeable future, if ever.

But where to find such myths is a question not easily answered.

It is tempting to look for them in the creeds of the established churches, to which the majority of us at least nominally belong. This, however, turns out to be of little use; since, as the propaganda leaflet to which I earlier alluded proudly and truly asserts, "All the major religions support organ and tissue donation." Indeed, the many sects and denominations of America (including the Roman Catholic, as the latest revision of their official Catechism makes clear) are less conflicted and divided on this issue than on such other ethically problematic medical procedures as euthanasia, abortion, and in vitro fertilization.

In any case, the myth systems to which we late twentieth-century Americans pay lip service on whatever our sabbaths may be are not the ones that determine our daily behavior—any more than the myths implicit in our politics, liberal or conservative (which, to make matters worse, tend finally to divide rather than unite an already heterogeneous, multi-ethnic society). The sole myth system that unites us all is to be found in Popular Culture, which constitutes in fact a kind of unsuspected secular scriptures. Certainly we are exposed to the archetypal images which it projects in print and post-print form for a much larger portion of our waking lives than we spend listening to sermons or political speeches. Moreover, precisely because we are not aware that we are being indoctrinated as we watch, listen, or read in quest of entertainment and escape, we are less apt to resist their implicit messages.

There is one subgenre of popular literature that deals centrally with technology, including the medical—and with the bioethical problems posed by its impact on our lives. This is, of course, science fiction, to which I am therefore tempted to turn first. But science fiction did not come into its own until the late 1920s, by which time the basic myths that trigger psychological rejection had already received their classic expression. Only quite recently have writers in that genre felt able to confront head-on the new procedures that have made organ and tissue transplantation available to a large number of patients—and consequently a topic of general interest.

Their stories, in any case, when they do not project juvenile fantasies about transplanted members taking control of their host bodies, tend to be more ideological than mythological. In fictions by highly esteemed writers in the genre (like Robert Silverberg's "Caught in the Organ Draft," or Larry Niven's "The Patchwork Girl" and "The Jigsaw Man"), transplantation is represented as a form of exploitation. Sometimes it is portrayed as being imposed on the powerless young by a dictatorial gerontocracy, eager to add to its other privileges that of indefinitely prolonged life. Sometimes it is described as a stratagem of the very rich, who seduce the desperately impoverished into selling their own flesh; or—where such sales are forbidden by law—hire criminals to rob the graves of anonymous paupers and kidnap, drug, even murder the living poor.

Both of these scenarios seem updated versions of familiar nineteenth-century tales about "Resurrection Men," the body-snatchers who provided corpses for dissection in anatomy classes of medical schools and hospitals. This time around, however, doctors, though villains still, are portrayed not as the instigators of such atrocities but merely as accomplices after the fact. In any case, these latter-day tales of "organ-legging" serve to foster similar fears and resentment of the medical profession—feeding a preexistent iatrophobia, which ever since the 1960s has been endemic in our society. To make matters worse, they have passed into the lore of the streets, in which they are reported as having actually happened. Occasionally, indeed, they do—chiefly in third world countries such as India—but even when the reports are apocryphal, they make it into supermarket scandal sheets, where, though in due course disproved, they are still believed by the credulous.

Nonetheless, no late twentieth century grave robber has as yet been mythicized like those of the last century—the notorious Burke and Hare, for instance. Nor, for that matter, have any of the characters in more recent science fiction entered our communal nightmares. Such mythological status has, however, been achieved by the protagonists of four popular novels, which still attract the mass audience and continue to haunt us, sleeping or waking.

The first of these, Mary Shelley's *Frankenstein,* was written when the nineteenth century had barely begun; and the other three, Bram Stoker's *Dracula,* Robert Louis Stevenson's *Dr. Jekyll and Mr. Hyde,* and H. G. Wells's *The Island of Dr. Moreau* in the last decades of that century—all of them, in other words, not only before transplantation had become viable but before "science fiction" as a genre had found a proper name and a distinctive identity. All four of them, though not quite science fiction, seem forerunners of that form at its most bleakly dystopian, but they more closely resemble a related but finally different genre, the Horror Story.

Beginning in England in the late eighteenth century with the Gothic Romance or Tale of Terror, and imported into this country by Edgar Allen Poe, such fictions have remained favorites of American readers down to the present day—most notoriously perhaps in the super best-sellers of Stephen King. Earlier examples of the form, however, typically seek to make us shudder by evoking the occult and supernatural; whereas three of the mythic books we are examining deal solely with what is, though terrifying, naturally explicable, and the fourth, *Dracula,* treats both.

What all four try to frighten us with are primarily the new horrors which have come to haunt us after the Age of Reason had presumably laid to rest forever all traditional demons and bugaboos. These are, of course, the horrors created by modern science and technology, particularly in the field of medicine—with whose procedures most of us sooner or later become all too familiar at first hand; since driven by pain and fear we entrust ourselves to such healers, even though their methods for averting death and prolonging life challenge our most dearly held beliefs about mortality and immortality. Small wonder then that in our most archetypal fictions, doctors tend to be portrayed as villains, who—having hubristically usurped the divine power to create and destroy—end by bringing disaster on themselves and those they hold most dear.

More specifically, Wells's Dr. Moreau is portrayed as attempting, with an utter disregard for the pain inflicted, to take the process of evolution into his own hands: turning beasts into men by vivisection, plastic surgery, and hypnosis. Stevenson's Dr. Jekyll, on the other hand, experiments only on himself, releasing by psycho-chemistry all the dark impulses we normally repress for the sake of civility; and simultaneously altering the fleshy envelope of his body, which his potion makes younger even as it turns it repulsive. In the end he is trapped in that body, becoming a serial murderer, whose last victim is himself.

Bram Stoker's *Dracula* seems at first glance anomalous in this regard, since though there are two doctors in the major dramatis personae, neither is identified as a villain. The first, Dr. Seward, a psychiatrist, however ineffectual is clearly on the side of good; while the second, Dr. Bram Van Helsing, is portrayed as the enemy of the villainous Vampire. On closer examination, however, Van Helsing turns out to be a disconcertingly ambiguous figure, as much an alter ego as an antagonist of that villain.

To begin with, he, too, is a stranger in a strange land, speaking English with a foreign accent. Moreover, though Van Helsing is introduced as "one of the most advanced scientists of the day," having (as we eventually learn) "revolutionized therapeutics by the discovery of the continuous evolution of brain matter," the only scientific means he uses to thwart the Vampire is blood transfusion. For the rest he depends on Old World charms and amulets like wreaths of garlic, crucifixes, Holy Water, and stakes driven through the heart. As a matter of fact, though one of Dracula's cognomens is "Vlad Teppish," Vlad the Impaler, it is the good doctor whom we actually see impaling the Vampire—as well as presiding over a similar ritual mutilation of Lucy Westenra, Vlad's first female victim. In any case, Van Helsing for the most part, quite like the foe he seeks to destroy, operates not in the realm of modern science but of ancient magic, black and white.

Even transfusion seems finally to belong to that realm, being like vampirism, an attempt to prolong life (the Vampire, after all, aims not to kill but to make "undead") by transferring vital fluids from one body to another. Additionally, as Stoker makes clear, the transfusions from multiple donors, including himself, which Van Helsing sets up in his earlier vain attempts to save Lucy, end by making her in a sense polyandrous. Like Dracula's later forcing of Mina (Lucy's friend and his second intended female victim) to drink from his veins, Van Helsing's therapeutic mingling of blood calls into question the sanctity of Christian marriage. He perpetrates, that is to say, a travesty of sexual union, which undercuts the orthodox belief that only a man and his wife can and should be made one flesh.

It seems to me quite evident, in any case, that Stoker's fantasy about the irruption of vampirism into the modern world was initially triggered by the invention of blood transfusion, which is, of course, the precursor of organ and tissue transplantation, along with the bioethical problems it poses. Stoker, however, does not deal with those problems, as explicitly as does Mary Shelley in *Frankenstein,* which—prophetically, as it were—confronted head-on the dark side of harvesting the body parts of the dead to prolong life. Her hyperbolic "fairy tale" was suggested, she informs us in her introduction, by an overheard conversation about recent experiments in which inert matter was revivified by the passage of an electric current. But in her actual text she never describes the process by which a patchwork of cadaveric parts is transformed into a living being.

What she does depict is the horror of digging up graves and dissecting corpses. Indeed, she does this twice over: once when she relates the creation of the original male monster and again when she tells how, in response to that monster's demand, Frankenstein begins to fabricate a mate for him. Though he rejects the first and never completes the second, Frankenstein pays dearly for both impious attempts to manufacture more-than-human creatures by what amounts to a total body transplant.

Nor does it mitigate his guilt that—as she makes clear from the very start—his motives are benign and his methods scientific. Old-fashioned necromancy, we learn early on, he has long since abandoned as delusory as well as evil. It is therefore in the university laboratory rather than the lairs of magicians that he seeks to discover "the cause and generation of life." And in this sense he is the prototype of the modern white-jacketed surgeon transplanting hearts and livers rather than the heir of alchemists searching for the *elixir vitae*.

To be sure, Mrs. Shelley never refers to Frankenstein as a "doctor"—calling him only "Victor" or "Baron." But in the popular mind he rapidly came to be thought of as, and has remained forever, "Dr." Frankenstein, his name without that honorific title having been attached instead to his monstrous creation, whom Mrs. Shelley left nameless. It seems a little surprising all the same that *Frankenstein* so deeply moved its readers long before the Hospital had become a major institution, the practice of medicine a prestigious and rewarding (though ambivalently regarded) profession, health care a large part of every national budget, and bioethics a subject of obsessive concern. But surely this is no more surprising than the fact that it, and the three other books with which I have linked it, have continued to do so; none of them has gone out of print to this very day, despite the changes of fashion in literature and lifestyle. After all, they are essentially mythic works, which is to say, they exist out of time, in the eternal now of the collective unconscious.

For the same reason, they have been felt from the very start as being in the public domain: the property not of their nominal authors but of the mass audience worldwide. Shortly after publication, they were translated into other media: first stage plays, then horror films, TV shows, and eventually comic strips and comic books. Finally, they have escaped from all media and are transmitted by word of mouth; the cognomens of their sinister protagonists turned into common nouns, familiar even to those who have never encountered their stories on the page or on the screen. This is less true of *The Island of Dr. Moreau* than of the others; but *Frankenstein* and *Dr. Jekyll and Mr. Hyde* have been thus transmogrified scores of times, while the versions of *Dracula* have reached the hundreds.

In the course of such metamorphoses, the names inscribed on their original title pages have typically been forgotten by most readers and viewers. Moreover, only a few of us are aware of how much else has been lost or added or radically changed in the process, not just style and structure, which is inevitable, but theme, plot, and character. Finally, however, even we happy few have to grant that it is right that these tales (once again, like all true myths) be stripped by the popular mind of all that it instinctively senses is extraneous, even as it fills in what it feels to be blanks. First of all, subthemes of the original texts that are ideological or personal rather than archetypal and universal tend to disappear in the later recessions. These include Bram Stoker's many allusions to new technologies of information storage and retrieval, as well as his references to the impact on traditional morality of the feminist movement of late Victorian times, Mary Shelley's repeated allusions to birthing and motherin,; and R. L. Stevenson's reflections on the oedipal encounter of fathers and sons.

Meanwhile, characters absent from the original dramatis personae have come to play important roles in the ever-developing myth. Especially notable among these are the sinister cripple, Igor, who serves as Frankenstein's lab assistant, the even more monstrous Bride who rejects his Monster—and the various female characters who have been added to the initially all-male cast of *Dr. Jekyll and Mr. Hyde* to provide occasions for romance or titillating sexual assaults. In addition, certain characters included from the start have drastically altered; the Monster himself, for instance, whom Mrs. Shelley imagined as fully literate and super-articulate in at least two languages, has become a stuttering analphabetic with bolts in his head.

What has remained untouched, however, or rather, what has become ever more clearly defined thanks to such changes is the mythological core of these tales. In it the archetypal Doctor is portrayed as an enemy (all the more dangerous because of his good intentions) of those traditional beliefs which long enabled us to live at peace with our fragile bodies and our sense of their inescapable mortality. Typically in a lonely setting, which symbolizes his alienation from the rest of humanity, that Doctor creates a creature intended to be better than his imperfect self, perhaps even immortal. Inevitably, though, that creature turns out to be a monster and his creator even more of one for having dared to usurp the prerogatives of a superhuman Creator. That archetypal scenario will, of course, continue to be imagined and reimagined for as long as humanity continues to fear death, call on science to forestall it, and resent it for doing so.

Moreover, just as the telling of that mythic tale has no foreseeable end, it has no discernible beginning. Indeed, one reason for the instant success of books like *Frankenstein* and *Dracula* is their readers' feeling that the tale they tell is one they have always known, without being quite able to formulate. Even in medieval and early modern times, when society still put its trust in magic rather than technology to conquer the ultimate horror of death, mythic stories embodying that horror and that trust were already being formulated—the best known of these being that of Dr. Faustus, which has come down to us in a play by Christopher Marlowe, and a long epic poem by Goethe, along with later plays and operas based largely on them.

That ill-fated experimenter not only succeeded in rejuvenating himself but created the homunculus, a living human being of miniature size. His methods, to be sure, were not medical (despite his title, he was a magus rather than an M.D.) but thaumaturgic, beginning with evoking malign spirits and culminating in a pact with the Devil. Something closer to the techniques of present-day science were practiced by the Alchemists, whose search for the Elixir of Life also became the subject of many-times-told tales. But though their art was the forerunner of modern chemistry, in their own time they, too, were also portrayed as Black Magicians risking damnation in a quest for forbidden knowledge.

In our time, however, when many of us have ceased to believe in damnation or indeed in any form of otherworldly life after death, the pursuit of immortality in this life has come to be regarded, on the conscious level, as a benign activity. On the one hand, research in cryonics and cloning is generously supported and the moribund provided, at great expense, with prosthetic devices, artificial life-support systems and, of course, transplanted organs, including the mythological heart itself. On the other hand, we are being constantly urged to avoid suspected carcinogens and foods high in cholesterol—including such longtime staples as tobacco and whiskey, coffee, sugar, eggs, and milk—even as we pop vitamin pills and rack our decaying bodies with dieting, jogging, and aerobics. It is as if we were secretly convinced (though we do not confess it openly) that one more food forbidden, one more exercise regime required, one more miracle drug or surgical procedure perfected will make us all live forever.

Nonetheless, at a deeper level of the psyche, the dark side of our old ambivalence about the quest for immortality keeps suggesting that perhaps this whole strategy is wrong, misguided—finally monstrous; that forestalling death indefinitely is as impious as hastening it was traditionally thought to be; that, in the eloquent words of Shakespeare: "We must endure our going hence even as our coming hither...the readiness is all..." Surely, such a conviction underlies the covert rejection of transplantation—not despite but precisely because of its success in prolonging life. So, at any rate, the mythic tales I have been examining would seem to be trying to tell us.

The Tyranny of the Normal

≫≪

I AM NOT A DOCTOR or a nurse or a social worker, confronted in my daily rounds with the problem of physical disability; not even a lawyer, philosopher, or theologian trained to deal with its moral and legal implications. I am only a poet, novelist, critic—more at home in the world of words and metaphor than fact, which is to say, an expert, if at all, in reality once removed. Yet despite this, I have been asked on numerous occasions to address groups of health-care professionals about this subject—no doubt because I once published a book called *Freaks: Myths and Images of the Secret Self.* In that book, I was primarily interested in exploring (as the subtitle declares) the fascination of "normals" with the sort of congenital malformations traditionally displayed at Fairs and Sideshows, and especially the way in which such freaks are simultaneously understood as symbols of the absolute Other and the essential Self. Yet in the long and difficult process of putting that study together (it took almost six years of my life and led me into dark places in my own psyche I was reluctant to enter), I stumbled inadvertently into dealing also with the subject of "the care of imperiled newborns."

How difficult and dangerous a topic this was I did not realize, however, until just before my book was due to appear. I was at a party celebrating the imminent event when I mentioned offhand to one of my fellow-celebrants, a young man who turned out to be an M.D., one of the discoveries I had made in the course of my research: that in all probability more "abnormal" babies were being allowed to die (in effect, being killed) in modern hospitals than had been in the Bad Old Days when they were exposed and left to perish by their fathers. And I went on to declare that in my opinion, at least, this was not good; at which point, my interlocutor screamed at me (rather contradictorily, I thought) that what I asserted was simply not true—and that, in any case, it was perfectly all right to do so. Then he hurled his Martini glass at the wall behind me and stalked out of the room.

He did not stay long enough for me to explain that our disagreement was more than merely personal, based on more than the traditional mutual distrust of the scientist and the humanist. Both of our attitudes, I wanted to tell him, had deep primordial roots: sources far below the level of our fully conscious values and the facile rationalizations by which we customarily defend them. It is, therefore, to certain ancient myths and legends that we must turn—and here my literary expertise stands me in good stead—to understand the roots of our deep ambivalence toward fellow creatures who are perceived at any given moment as disturbingly deviant, outside currently acceptable physiological norms. That ambivalence has traditionally impelled us toward two quite different responses to the "monsters" we beget. On the one hand, we have throughout the course of history killed them—ritually at the beginning, as befits divinely sent omens of disaster, portents of doom. On the other hand, we have sometimes worshiped them as if they were themselves divine, though never without overtones of fear and repulsion. In either case, what prompted our response was a sense of wonder and awe: a feeling that such "unnatural" products of the natural process by which we continue the species are mysterious, uncanny, finally "taboo."

Though it may not be immediately evident, the most cursory analysis reveals that not only have that primitive wonder and awe persisted into our "scientific," secular age, but so also have the two most archaic ways of expressing it. In the first place, we continue to kill, or at least allow to die, monstrously malformed neonates. We euphemize the procedure, however, disguise the superstitious horror at its roots, by calling what we do "the removal of life supports from nonviable *terata*" (*terata* being Greek for "monster"). Moreover, thanks to advanced medical techniques, we can do better these days than merely fail to give malformed preemies a fair chance to prove whether or not they are really "viable." We can detect and destroy before birth, babies likely to be born deformed; even abort them wholesale when the occasion arises, as in the infamous case of the Thalidomide babies of the sixties. That was a particularly unsavory episode (which we in this country were spared), since the phocomelic infants, carried by mothers dosed with an antidote prescribed for morning sickness, were in the full sense of the word "iatrogenic freaks." And the doctors who urged their wholesale abortion (aware that less than half of them would prove to be deformed, but why take chances?) were in many cases the very ones who had actually prescribed the medication.

To be sure, those responsible for such pre-infanticide did not confess—were not even aware, though any poet could have told them—that they were motivated by vestigial primitive fears of abnormality, exacerbated by their guilt at having caused it. They sought only, they assured themselves and the rest of the world, to spare years of suffering to the doomed children and their parents; as well as to alleviate the financial burden on those parents and the larger community, which would have to support them through what promised to be a nonproductive lifetime. We do, however, have at this point records of the subsequent lives of some of the Thalidomide babies whose parents insisted on sparing them (a wide-ranging study was made some years later in Canada), which turned out to have been, from their own point of view, at least, neither notably nonproductive, nor especially miserable. None of them, at any rate, were willing to confess that they would have wished themselves dead.

But such disconcerting facts do not faze apologists for such drastic procedures. Nor does the even more dismaying fact that the most wholehearted, full-scale attempt at teratacide occurred in Hitler's Germany, with the collaboration, by the way, of not a few quite respectable doctors and teratologists, most notably a certain Etienne Wolff of the University of Strasbourg. Not only were dwarfs and other "useless people" sent to Nazi extermination camps and parents adjudged "likely" to beget anomalous children sterilized; but other unfortunate human beings regarded—at that time and in that society—as undesirable deviations from the Norm were also destroyed: Jews and Gypsies first of all, with Blacks, Slavs and Mediterraneans presumably next in line. It is a development which should make us aware of just how dangerous enforced physiological normality is when the definition of its parameters falls into the hands of politicians and bureaucrats. And into what other hands can we reasonably expect it to fall in any society we know or can imagine in the foreseeable future?

Similarly, even as the responsibility for the ritual slaughter of Freaks was passing from the family to the State, the terrified adoration of Freaks was passing from the realm of worship to that of entertainment and art. To be sure, the adoration of Freaks in the Western world was never a recognized religion but at best an underground Cult. Think, for instance, of the scene in Fellini's *Satyricon*, in which a Hermaphrodite is ritually displayed to a group of awestricken onlookers, who regard him as more than a curiosity, though not quite a god: after all, the two reigning myth-systems of our culture, the Hellenic and the Judaeo-Christian, both disavowed the portrayal of the divine in freakish guise, regarding as barbarous or pagan the presentation of theriomorphic, two-headed, or multi-limbed divinities.

Yet there would seem always to have been a hunger in all of us, a need to behold in quasi-religious wonder our mysteriously anomalous brothers and sisters. For a long time, this need was satisfied in Courts for the privileged few, at fairs and sideshows for the general populace, by collecting and exhibiting Giants, Dwarfs, Intersexes, Joined Twins, Fat Ladies, and Living Skeletons. Consequently, even in a world that grew ever more secular and rational, we could still continue to be baffled, horrified, and moved by Freaks, as we were able to be by fewer and fewer other things once considered most sacred and terrifying. Finally though, the Sideshow began to die, even as the rulers of the world learned to be ashamed of their taste for human "curiosities." By then, however, their images had been preserved in works of art, in which their implicit meanings are made manifest.

Walk through the picture galleries of any museum in the western world and you will find side by side with the portraits of Kings and Courtesans depictions of the Freaks they once kept to amuse them, by painters as distinguished as Goya and Velasquez. Nor has the practice died out in more recent times, carried on by artists as different as Currier and Ives (who immortalized such stars of P. T. Barnum's sideshow as General Tom Thumb) and Pablo Picasso (who once spent more than a year painting over and over in ever shifting perspectives the dwarfs who first appeared in Velasquez's *Las Meninas*). Nor did other popular forms of representation abandon that intriguing subject. Not only have photographers captured on film the freaks of their time, but after a while they were portrayed in fiction as well. No sooner, in fact, had the novel been invented, than it too began to portray the monstrous and malformed as objects of pity and fear and—however secularized— wonder, always wonder. Some authors of the nineteenth century, indeed, seem so freak-haunted that remembering them, we remember first of all the monsters they created. We can scarcely think of Victor Hugo, for instance, without recalling his grotesque Hunchback of Notre Dame, any more than we can recall Charles Dickens without thinking of his monstrous dwarf, Quilp, or our own Mark Twain without remembering "Those Incredible Twins." And the tradition has been continued by postmodernists like John Barth and Donald Barthelme and Vladimir Nabakov, who, turning their backs on almost all the other trappings of the conventional novel, still reflect its obsession with Freaks.

In the twentieth century, the images of congenital malformations are, as we might expect, chiefly preserved in the artform it invented, the cinema: on the one hand, in Art Films intended for a select audience of connoisseurs, like the surreal fantasies of Fellini and Ingmar Bergman; and on the other, in a series of popular movies from Todd Browning's thirties' masterpiece, *Freaks,* to the more recent *Elephant Man,* in its various versions. Browning's extraordinary film was by no means an immediate success; in fact, it horrified its earliest audience and first critics, who drove it from the screen and its director into early retirement. But it was revived in the sixties and has since continued to be replayed all over the world, particularly in colleges and universities. And this seems especially appropriate, since in the course of filming his fable of the Freaks' revenge on their "normal" exploiters, Browning gathered together the largest collection of showfreaks ever assembled in a single place: an immortal Super-Sideshow, memorializing a popular artform on the verge of disappearing along with certain congenital malformations it once "starred" (but that are now routinely "repaired"), like Siamese Twins.

For this reason, perhaps, we are these days particularly freak-obsessed, as attested also by the recent success of *The Elephant Man* on stage and TV and at the neighborhood movie theatre. The central fable of that parabolic tale, in which a Doctor, a Showman, the Press, and the Public contend for the soul of a freak, though the events on which it is based happened in Victorian times, seems especially apposite to our present ambivalent response to human abnormality, reminding us of what we now otherwise find it difficult to confess except in our REM sleep: that those wretched caricatures of our idealized body image, which at first appear to represent the absolutely "Other" (thus reassuring us who come to gape that we are "normal") are really a revelation of what in our deepest psyches we recognize as the Secret Self. After all, not only do we know that each of us is a freak to someone else; but in the depths of our unconscious (where the insecurities of childhood and adolescence never die) we seem forever freaks to ourselves.

The Tyranny of the Normal

Perhaps it is especially important for us to realize that *there are no normals,* at a moment when we are striving desperately to eliminate freaks, to normalize the world. This misguided impulse represents a third, an utterly new response to the mystery of human anomalies—made possible for the first time by modern medical technology and sophisticated laboratory techniques. Oddly enough (and to me terrifyingly), it proved possible for such experimental scientists to produce monsters long before they learned to prevent or cure them. To my mind, therefore, the whole therapeutic enterprise is haunted by the ghosts of those two-headed, three-legged, one-eyed chicks and piglets taht the first scientific teratologists of the eighteenth century created and destroyed in their laboratories.

Nonetheless, I do not consider those first experimenters with genetic mutation my enemies, for all their deliberate profanation of a mystery dear to the hearts of the artists with whom I identify. Nor would I be presumptuous, heartless enough to argue—on esthetic or even moral grounds—that congenital malformations under no circumstances be "repaired," or if need be, denied birth, to spare suffering to themselves or others. I am, however, deeply ambivalent on this score for various reasons, some of which I have already made clear, and others of which I will now try to elucidate. I simply do not assume (indeed, the burden of evidence indicates the contrary) that being born a freak is per se an unendurable fate. As I learned reading scores of biographies of such creatures in the course of writing my book about them, the most grotesque among them have managed to live lives neither notably worse nor better than that of most humans. They have managed to support themselves at work which they enjoyed (including displaying themselves to the public); they have loved and been loved, married and begot children—sometimes in their own images, sometimes not.

More often than not, they have survived and coped; sometimes, indeed, with special pride and satisfaction because of their presumed "handicaps," which not a few of them have resisted attempts to "cure." Dwarfs in particular have joined together to fight for their "rights," one of which they consider to be *not* having their size brought up by chemotherapy and endocrine injections to a height we others call "normal," but that they refer to, less honorifically, as "average." And I must say I sympathize with their stand, insofar as the war against "abnormality" implies a dangerous kind of politics, which beginning with a fear of difference, eventuates in a tyranny of the Normal. That tyranny, moreover, is sustained by creating in those outside the Norm shame and self-hatred—particularly if they happen to suffer from those "deformities" (which are still the vast majority) that we cannot prevent or cure.

Reflecting on these matters, I cannot help remembering not only the plight of the Jews and Blacks under Hitler but the situation of the same ethnic groups—more pathetic-comic than tragic, but deplorable all the same—here in supposedly non-totalitarian America merely a generation or two ago. At that point, many Blacks went scurrying off to their corner pharmacy in quest of skin bleaches and hair straighteners; and Jewish women with proud semitic beaks turned to cosmetic surgeons for nose jobs. To be sure, as the example of Barbra Streisand makes clear, we have begun to deliver ourselves from the tyranny of such ethnocentric Norms in the last decades of the twentieth century; so that looking Niggerish or Kike-ish no longer seems as freakish as it once did, and the children of "lesser breeds" no longer eat their hearts out because they do not look like Dick and Jane, the WASP-lets portrayed in their Primers.

But the Cult of Slimness, that aberration of Anglo-Saxon taste (no African or Slav or Mediterranean ever believed in his homeland that "no one can be too rich or too thin") still prevails. And joined with the Cult of Eternal Youth, it has driven a population growing ever older and fatter to absurd excesses of jogging, dieting, and popping amphetamines—or removing with the aid of plastic surgery those stigmata of time and experience once considered worthy of reverence. Nor do things stop there; since the skills of the surgeon are now capable of recreating our bodies in whatever shape whim and fashion may decree as esthetically or sexually desirable: large breasts and buttocks at one moment, meagre ones at another. By why *not,* after all? If in the not-so-distant future, the grosser physiological abnormalities that have for so long haunted us disappear forever—prevented, repaired, aborted, or permitted to die at birth—those of us allowed to survive by the official enforcers of the Norm will be free to become ever more homogeneously, monotonously beautiful; which is to say, supernormal, however that ideal may be defined. And who except some nostalgic poet, in love with difference for its own sake, would yearn for a world where ugliness is still possible? Is it not better to envision and work for one where all humans are at last *really* equal—physiologically as well as socially and politically?

But, alas (and this is what finally gives me pause), it is impossible for all of us to achieve this dubious democratic goal—certainly not in the context of our society as it is now and promises to remain in the foreseeable future: a place in which supernormality is to be had not for the asking but only for the buying (cosmetic surgery, after all, is not included in Medicare). What seems probable, therefore, as a score of science-fiction novels have already prophesied, is that we are approaching with alarming speed a future in which the rich and privileged will have as one more, ultimate privilege the hope of a surgically, chemically, hormonally induced and preserved normality—with the promise of immortality by organ transplant just over the horizon. And the poor (who, we are assured on good authority, we always have with us) will be our sole remaining Freaks.

Acknowledgments

Acknowledgment is made to the following publications in which these essays first appeared, sometimes in slightly different form and under slightly different titles:

"The Rebirth of God and the Death of Man": *Salmagundi* (winter 1973).

"Pity and Fear": *Salmagundi* (summer 1982).

"Eros and Thanatos": *Salmagundi* (summer-fall 1977).

"More Images of Eros and Old Age": *Memory and Desire: Aging–Literature–Psychoanalysis*, ed. by Kathleen Woodward and Murray M. Schwartz (Bloomington: Indiana University Press, 1986).

"Child Abuse": *Children's Literature*, v. 8 (New Haven: Yale University Press, 1980).

"Images of the Doctor": Previously unpublished speech.

"Images of the Nurse": *Literature and Medicine: Images of Healers*, v. 2, ed. by Anne Hudson Jones (Albany: State University of New York Press, 1983).

"Why Organ Transplant Programs Do Not Succeed": *Organ Transplantation: Meanings and Realities*, ed. by Stuart J. Youngner, Renée C. Fox, and Laurence J. O'Connell (Madison: University of Wisconsin Press, 1996).

"The Tyranny of the Normal": *The Hastings Center Report* (special supplement: "On the Care of Imperiled Newborns"), v. 14, n. 2 (April 1984).

About the Author

LESLIE FIEDLER WAS born in Newark, New Jersey, in 1917. He did his undergraduate work at New York University and received his M.A. and PH.D. from the University of Wisconsin. After teaching at Montana State University for over two decades, during which time he served as Chairman of the Department of English from 1954 to 1956, he became Professor of English at the State University of New York at Buffalo, where he holds the Samuel L. Clemens Chair in English. He has been honored with numerous grants and awards including a Rockefeller Fellowship and two Fulbright Fellowships. In 1988 he was elected to the American Academy of Arts and Letters. Most recently, Fiedler received The Chancellor Charles P. Norton Medal, awarded by SUNY at Buffalo. He is the author of twenty-five books.

Tyranny of the Normal

was set in Fairfield, a slightly decorative old-style face originally designed for Linotype by the American graphic designer and wood engraver Rudolph Ruzicka. Sharply cut, as if by an artist's graver rather than a pen, Fairfield was designed to invite continuous reading. It illustrates Ruzicka's conviction that type should "have a subtle degree of interest and variety of design."